New Essentials for Teaching Reading in PreK–2

PAULA MOORE and ANNA LYON

Foreword by Gay Su Pinnell

■SCHOLASTIC

NEW YORK • TORONTO • LONDON • AUCKLAND • SYDNEY
MEXICO CITY • NEW DELHI • HONG KONG • BUENOS AIRES

Dedication

We dedicate this book to our parents who taught us the value of reading for enjoyment and learning.

To my mother, Charline Hawkensen Ferren who taught
me how to imagine the crisp mountain air of the
Alps and the buttery taste of the goat cheese that we
read about in her own cherished copy of the book,
Heidi, by Johanna Spyri (undated), which I still have.
To my father, Roland Ferren, who taught me to value
education and who provided a model for hard work
and perseverance.

Paula Moore

To my mother, Lacy Raleigh Turner, for her lesson that
girls are strong and capable.
To my father, Wilgus Turner, for his unwavering
support and for being my biggest fan.

Anna Lyon

Page 46: From PRINCESS FURBALL by Charlotte Huck. Copyright © 1980 by Charlotte Huck. Published by Greenwillow, a division of HarperCollins; Page 55: From THE EDUCATOR'S WORD FREQUENCY GUIDE. Published by Touchstone Applied Associates Inc., 1995; Page 62: Curriculum-Based norms in Oral reading Fluency for Grade 2; by J.E. Hasbrouck and G. Tindal from Teaching Exceptional Children, 24, 41–44; Page 131: From MRS. WISHY-WASHY by Joy Cowley. Copyright © 1990 by Joy Cowley. Published by Philomel Books; Page 133: From SALLY'S FRIENDS by Beverley Randell. Published by Rigby, 1994; Page 136: From ALL ABOUT FROGS by Jim Arnosky. Copyright © 2002 by Jim Arnosky. Published by Scholastic Inc.

Cover design by Maria Lilja; Cover photo by © Photodisc Blue

Interior design by Ellen Matlach for Boultinghouse & Boultinghouse, Inc.

Interior photographs: © Joe Cornish/Stone/GETTY IMAGES, 107; © Digital Vision/GETTY IMAGES, 71; © Britt Erlanson/The Image Bank/GETTY IMAGES, 25; © Michael Krasowitz/Taxi/GETTY IMAGES, 39; James Levin, 7, 51, 89; Maria Lilja, 143; © Photodisc/GETTY IMAGES, 79; © Barry Rosenthal/Taxi/GETTY IMAGES, 123; Ellen Senisi, 15; all others courtesy of the authors.

ISBN 0-439-62368-5

2 3 4 5 6 7 8 9 10   23   12 11 10 09 08 07

Contents

Acknowledgments

We would like to thank four important groups of people who have made major contributions to our work in different ways. First, during the writing of this book and in all other scholarly endeavors, we have enjoyed the support of many fine colleagues. They have challenged our thinking and encouraged us to take chances. Gay Su Pinnell, Carol Lyons, Irene Fountas, Andrea McCarrier, Ellen Almquist, Linda Dorn, Mary Lose, Rosemary Bamford, Janice Kristo, Carolyn Ledford, Susan Colby, Jeff Wilhelm, Jane Wellman-Little, and Susan Taylor have all provided us with unselfish support and guidance.

Second, we are forever grateful and deeply indebted to the classroom teachers who have shared their wisdom and allowed us access to their children. Snow Hill Primary, Pactolus Elementary, ECU's Child Development Laboratory, Old Town Elementary School, and Vine Street School all graciously opened their doors to us. Kelly Berube, Shelly Tennett, Shanna Curtis, Kelly Mead, Dianne Johnson, Becky Smith, Debbie Swett, Sandy Daniel, Vickie Sutton, Melissa Rees, Kathy Harrell, Kathy Grantham, Heather Wiggins, Amy Cobb, Linda Harrell, Alena Esposito, and Cindy Beaman have taught us a great deal. We are pleased to learn from and to teach with them. They, and many other teachers too numerous to list here, have offered valuable insights and kept us grounded in the everyday realities of life in the classroom. We'd like to extend a special thank you to Lynn Coy-Ogen, Sharon Greaney, Jeanna Tuelle, and Chris Avila who have all shared their leadership strategies for guiding literacy-focused initiatives in schools.

Third, we would like to acknowledge the excellent work of the editorial team at Scholastic, and in particular, Virginia Dooley and Margery Rosnick, who have stayed with us through the ups and downs of publishing. They were exceptionally generous with their time, resources, advice, and support and always made us feel good about our writing.

And, last but not least, our families have shared our frustrations and tolerated our long hours of writing in seclusion. They have kept our lives running smoothly and have kept us encouraged. Our husbands, Don Moore and Virgil Lyon, have proven their commitment to us and to the work we do. Our children, Carl, Amy, James, Virgil, and Leah, have kept us going with their pride in our work. And finally, to Matthew, Ben, Collin, Eddie, Simon, Sierra, and all of the little ones in our lives, thank you for providing us with honest examples of childhood.

Foreword

by
Gay Su Pinnell

In *New Essentials for Teaching Reading in PreK–2*, Paula Moore and Anna Lyon have produced a book for today's teaching. They explore the terrains of comprehension, fluency, and vocabulary learning across many instructional contexts and provide an accessible review of research on each of these important topics. Their work will be helpful to teachers in breaking down complex areas such as word learning, meaning-making, and language processing, and teasing out important information and ideas. In the first part of the book, the authors discuss the research foundation, and in the second part of the book they move us into the world of the classroom. This book is peppered with engaging examples from children, parents, grandparents, and teachers.

For me, the book offered three very important and powerful ideas that have relevance for our work in literacy education. The first is that comprehending is a process rather than a product. As these authors describe this complex process, we realize that meaning-making is going on all the time—before, during, and after reading. As teachers we are concerned about nurturing meaning-making from the beginnings of literacy learning. Moore and Lyon describe how you can support the comprehending process, even among very young children as you engage in rich conversations across interactive read-alouds, shared reading, and interactive writing. They treat instruction in comprehending and fluency as intentional, yet describe a "light touch." They invite children to wonder about what they are reading. Instruction is embedded within authentic experiences with text. The conversations shown here are not about comprehension; rather, children engage in comprehending by entering into genuine talk about books.

The second important idea is that reading and writing emerge from meaningful talk. The authors emphasize oral language learning, presenting ideas from research that influence our decision making as we plan for and provide instruction. They also describe a wide range of ways to foster language development across the curriculum, with illustrative vignettes to help you think about the language environment of your classroom. As you read

New Essentials for Teaching Reading in PreK–2, you will find yourself thinking about the conversations that you have shared with your own students. The research-based information included here will affirm your commitment to reading aloud and discussing quality literature as a vital component of your instruction in comprehending, vocabulary, and fluency.

Third, the authors offer some provocative ideas that invite us to reflect on our own practice. You may have had the experience in your own school of engaging with your colleagues in a professional discussion of a book. It's very rewarding! Or, you may be reading this book on your own. If so, your own reflection will help you think constructively about your practice. The authors of this book take very seriously the role of the teacher and the teacher's decision making. That is not surprising since they have been involved in Reading Recovery, an early intervention program that provides extensive training of teachers and has had remarkable results for young, struggling readers and in Literacy Collaborative, a comprehensive literacy project that involves school staff members in working together to achieve school-wide excellence in literacy achievement. Both of these initiatives focus on teacher decision making and its role in achieving student success.

This book will help teachers provide both explicit instruction and highly supportive social contexts within which students learn not only the processes but the purposes of literacy in today's society.

Teaching Comprehension, Vocabulary, and Fluency

A New Emphasis in PreK–2

As primary-grade teachers, we want our students to become active, engaged readers. We want them to be motivated to listen to and read a variety of texts and use a repertoire of strategies to construct meaning. We want to hear them giggle when they read Shel Silverstein's poetry and Jon Scieszka's humorous transformations of traditional fairy tales. We want to hear them express their emotions when they read Eve Bunting's *Wednesday's Surprise* or *Fly Away Home.* We want to see their looks of amazement as they read Seymour Simon's *Wolves* or Gail Gibbon's *Sea Turtles.* We want to see their faces bursting with pride as they read sentences and stories they have written or share their ideas in discussion. Helping students to become active, strategic readers is a challenging process, but to be successful, one aspect is clear: We need to teach comprehension skills and strategies right from the start.

—Maureen McLaughlin

Anna and her three-year-old grandson, Ben, settle into the rocking chair for their nightly bedtime story. Anna pauses momentarily to fasten Ben's pajama top. Anxious to get on with his favorite book, *Brown Bear, Brown Bear, What Do You See?* by Bill Martin, Jr. (Holt, 1996), Ben tugs impatiently on Anna's arm, points to the words in the open book, and urgently demands, "Grandma, talk!"

Ben has not yet started preschool, but he is already developing meaning-making systems for comprehending written text. First, he expects that the books Grandma reads to him will bring enjoyment, wonder, and new learning, all the things that comprehending a written text provide. His grandmother has been reading to him since birth, and he has a large collection of favorite books in his toy box as well as on a special shelf on the bookcase in Grandma's living room. When they go on trips in the car, Ben entertains himself in his car seat, turning pages and "reading" his favorite parts. He loves getting a new book as a present, and he won't settle down until someone reads it to him.

Second, as Ben listens he uses comprehension strategies common to readers, such as predicting outcomes, anticipating events, distinguishing important ideas, and drawing inferences. These strategies help him understand and discuss the books with important people in his life. As each page in the book is turned, Ben smugly announces his prediction about which character will be seen next. When Grandma reads new books, he asks questions and comments on characters' actions, on pictures, and on the way language sounds. For example, Anna and Ben read *Chickens* by Diane Snowball (Mondo, 1995), an engaging little book that takes the reader through the egg-laying stages and ends with another grown hen on the last page. Ben turned back to the first page to look at the first grown hen and quizzed his grandma, "Same?" Already, Ben is demonstrating his ability to wonder about and question the text, a key comprehending process, as you will see in Chapter 2.

And third, Ben has made the link between spoken and written language systems, an important leap in beginning reading acquisition: He knows the story is in the text, not just the picture, and he knows that there is a match between speech and print because reading aloud sounds like "talk." If Grandma skips a page by mistake, Ben quickly corrects her and returns to the missed page, again demanding that she "talk." He delights in turning each page of *Brown Bear, Brown Bear, What Do You See?* and gleefully chiming in on the familiar refrain, "What do you see?"

Ben's early learning is providing him with a firm foundation for making sense of the world around him; it has also provided him with a foundation for listening to and comprehending the books Grandma reads to him—books he will eventually read himself. Shouldn't Ben's teachers continue building on this foundation for comprehending when he goes to school? The research supports doing so (e.g., National Institute of Child Health and Human Development [NICHHD], 2000a; Snow, Burns, & Griffin, 1998), but unfortunately, the conventional wisdom in the past was to teach for phonics first in the early grades, and comprehending processes later.

New Support for Teaching Comprehension, Vocabulary, and Fluency in PreK–2

Katherine Stahl wrote in an April 2004 article for *Reading Teacher*:

> **Until recently, I believed that my job as a first- or second-grade teacher was to develop fluent readers with the ability to decode novel text automatically. This would put them in good stead for comprehension instruction in the intermediate grades. This is no longer enough. (p. 598)**

When we were first- and second-grade teachers, we also felt the pressure to focus on decoding and phonics, the "sound systems" for reading. The implicit and explicit message from our curriculum directors and the commercial reading programs was that instruction for comprehension, vocabulary, and fluency, the "meaning-making systems," would begin in earnest in third grade, after children had learned "how to read."

That has all changed now. Most experts on early literacy development (e.g., Cole, 2003, 2004; McLaughlin, 2003; NICHHD, 2000a; Snow et al., 1998; Stahl, 2004) suggest that instruction in decoding and meaning-making systems should begin in tandem in all early literacy contexts, preschool through second grade. Anne Sweet and Catherine Snow sum up the new perspective in their chapter called "Reconceptualizing Reading Comprehension" for the IRA publication *Improving Comprehension Instruction* (2002):

> **Reading comprehension is usually a focus of instruction in the post-primary grades, after students have largely mastered word-recognition skills, though comprehension of text should be an integral part of reading instruction with beginning readers as well; and instruction in oral language, vocabulary, and listening comprehension should be a focus starting in preschool and throughout the elementary grades. (p. 23)**

In addition, the recent report by the National Reading Panel (NICHHD, 2000a) suggests that five research-based factors are critical for successful reading acquisition in the primary grades. Two of the factors are related to sound systems in reading: 1) phonemic awareness and 2) phonics. The other three factors are those critical for meaning-making in reading: 3) comprehension, 4) vocabulary, and 5) fluency.

> **Five Research-Based Factors Critical for Successful Reading Acquisition in the Primary Grades**
>
> 1. Phonemic awareness
> 2. Phonics
> 3. Comprehension
> 4. Vocabulary
> 5. Fluency

What This Book Is About

This book is an introduction to the meaning-making systems of comprehension, vocabulary, and fluency—how they are closely interrelated and why they are critical areas for instruction in the early years. It provides research-based information about how to teach comprehension, vocabulary, and fluency through the instructional contexts already present in most early literacy classrooms: read-alouds, shared reading, guided reading, interactive writing, writing workshop, and nonfiction content units. Instruction in comprehension, vocabulary, and fluency does not have to be layered on top of what you already do. It can be integrated into your current instruction with a little extra thought and planning.

Throughout the book, talk is presented as a powerful tool for teaching and a vehicle for learning. And we do mean *talk*, not lecture. Talk in the primary schools is a conversation, a give-and-take between two or more participants, in a social interaction that involves teaching and learning. In this book you will see teachers and children talking together about books, about experiences at learning centers, and about content-area explorations. Teachers talk to children to help them explore their understanding of concepts, words, experiences, and books.

How the Book Is Organized

Learning to read is complex because many components of the meaning-making process must occur simultaneously. Here are just a few of these components:

- recognizing words (fluency *and* vocabulary)

- deciding on the correct meaning of a word for the particular context (vocabulary *and* comprehension)

- grouping words into grammatical units (oral language knowledge *and* fluency)

- generating inferences (comprehending)

- using prior knowledge to construct a coherent, understandable model of the text (comprehending)

As you can see, it is hard to separate comprehension, vocabulary, and fluency either in describing them or in teaching young children. However, for convenience in writing about them, we have devoted two chapters to each of the topics. In Part I, Comprehension, Vocabulary, and Fluency Research, we give you a brief overview of the current research and theory about comprehension, vocabulary, and fluency development in young children. A major emphasis throughout these chapters is on how teachers use oral language and classroom talk to continue the development of meaning-making systems for comprehending written language.

Then, in Part II, Research Into Practice, you will see how comprehension, vocabulary, and fluency are addressed during instruction to help young readers build integrated meaning-making systems for reading and understanding text. We provide examples of research-based instruction in early literacy classrooms, preK through second grade. Our intent in these chapters is to capture instruction as it is integrated into typical contexts for early literacy instruction and to show how it changes over time in response to children's development.

♦ ♦ ♦ Final Thoughts ♦ ♦ ♦

Oral language itself is a major focus for instruction in early literacy contexts, as well as the vehicle through which comprehension, vocabulary, and fluency for reading are developed. Through talk and socializing interactions, young children learn the critical skills of literacy. In fact, language and literacy development continue to influence each other throughout life.

Judith Wells Lindfors (1991) says in her book about children's language and learning:

> **Language is inextricably entwined with our mental life—our perceiving, our remembering, our attending, our comprehending, our thinking—in short, all of our attempts to make sense of our experience in the world. (p. 8)**

language
✳

It is through language that our young students encounter a wider world in school and beyond than they have known at home. Through talk and print, they interact with others about new ideas, knowledge, and feelings. Therefore, we turn to the subject of talk in Chapter 1.

PART I

Comprehension, Vocabulary, and Fluency Research

The Role of Talk

The Research on Talk and Instruction

It is through the child's own talk and writing that he often 'encounters' and shapes his own ideas. Language enables the child to make his idea into a *thing*, an object, an entity that he can refine, consider, shape, and act on, much as he might act on clay. As with clay, the child can shape and *reshape*—can play with possibilities, can explore alternatives, can create new worlds of his own mind.

—Judith Wells Lindfors

One October afternoon, Cheryl Turner's kindergarten students are deeply involved in an interactive writing lesson. The children have decided on the text for the book they are making about the witch's brew and have chosen to add the sentence *In go the snakes*. The children are thinking about the word *snakes*. They are saying the word slowly and are listening for sounds. Samantha has been selected to write the *s*. She has written the letter backward and Cheryl is demonstrating how to make an *s*. The other children are looking on the name chart to see who else has an *s* in their name.

As Samantha makes her second attempt at an *s*, Justin notices the names of the teacher and the assistant. "Look," Justin says, "you both have *M-M, r-r, s-s*." The class checks and confirms Justin's observations. "Five people in our class have an *s* in their name," remarks Kristin. "We have Samantha, Justin, Jason, Casey, and me." Kristin goes to the name chart and points to each *s*.

Meanwhile, during Samantha's third attempt to write an *s*, she writes a *3* instead. "She wrote a *3*," says Jason. Not wanting to hurt his classmate's feeling, he quickly adds, "It's a very nice *3*." Samantha smiles. "Yes," says Cheryl, "Samantha wrote a very nice *3*, but that's not going to help us here. To write the word *snake*, we need an *s*." Cheryl guides Samantha's hand and together they make an *s*.

With the teacher's support, the children completed the word *snake*. Some children were ready to add a period, but others weren't so sure. The illustration the children had completed before coming to the writing lesson, showed one snake going into the pot. Some of the children wanted to keep the original sentence, *In go the snakes*, while others wanted to remain true to the illustration. After much discussion, the group decided to keep the original sentence because they thought it sounded better. Those concerned with the illustration decided that there could be other snakes already in the pot.

By listening to the children, Cheryl knows what the children are thinking about, what they are noticing, and what misunderstandings they may have. Gordon Wells (1986) tells us, "In early education, it is an oft-repeated slogan that one should 'start where the child is' . . . And what better way of knowing where they are than by listening to what they have to say" (p. 101). Cheryl knows, and the children in her class have discovered, that talk is a valuable tool for helping children learn to read and write.

Overview of the Chapter

This chapter includes a review of various theories of language development that researchers have proposed since the beginning of the twentieth century. It also includes brief summaries of the stages of language development. And finally we discuss the functions, value, and instructional purposes of talk.

Language Development

When young children learn to speak, we not only assume they will attach meaning to words, we encourage it. As soon as a child begins to name objects, we confirm his or her use of words and their meanings. Approximations are celebrated and encouraged. When a child says *ba-ba*, we understand this as an attempt to say the word *bottle*.

We often gesture and point while naming an object. "Ball," we say, while holding it for the child to see and touch. We add to current understandings with statements such as "big ball" or "red ball." Sentences are completed for the child. "Yes," we might say, "this is a big red ball."

It is a given that children are attempting to communicate by attaching meaning to speech. Adult caregivers go to great lengths to assist in this stage of language development. As young children become preschoolers, teachers continue the focus on talk and meaning. Activities are designed to not only assist children as they learn concepts but also help children acquire the related language. Preschool classrooms are filled with productive chatter. In elementary school classrooms, formal vocabulary instruction begins. Let's look closely at what researchers have had to say about language development.

What the Research Says About . . .
Language Development

Language development is a much-studied topic. Up until the 1950s B. F. Skinner and other behaviorists prevailed. They suggested that young children learned by imitating the language of others (1957). They believed that as the attempts were praised and reinforced, the child's speech grew and improved. Nativists, such as Noam Chomsky, disagreed with this view. They believed that humans were born with a set of rules about language in their brains; that they were "hardwired" to learn language (1969). Even with minimal outside assistance, children do learn to speak.

Language delays?

Jean Piaget's cognitive development theory states that children learn through activities (1955). Their initial language is about themselves and what they are doing. Most now believe in the constructivist theories (Brown, Cazden, & Bellugi-Klima, 1968), which are based on the ideas of Piaget and Lev Vygotsky. Constructivists believe that children develop language based on a set of innate concepts. In addition, they believe that language development is an active, social process; children can only use linguistic structures when they fully understand the concepts surrounding them.

While there is still much to be learned about language development, we do know that children go through fairly predictable stages as they learn to talk. During their first year, babies babble, usually combining consonant and vowel sounds (*ma*, *da*), and will repeat the same sound over and over again. Toward the end of their first year, many babies will speak their first word. Oral language grows a great deal between one and two years of age. Their repertoire includes one-word utterances not always understandable to adults. Telegraphic speech (nouns and verbs without function words, "More cookie," for example) develops next. Once the child begins to combine words, language grows rapidly. There is usually an explosion of language learning between ages two and three. Telegraphic speech continues, but syntactically complex sentences begin to develop.

By the time children are four years old, they have learned the basics of adult speech, and by the time they are seven, they have control of most adult grammar. Seven- and eight-year-olds are capable of true conversation; they can respond intelligently to statements made by others and can further the conversation by adding new information and ideas to the topic at hand. Seven-year-old Lauren and her dad were looking for a lost puzzle piece. Lauren's father suggested using her flashlight to look in dark places such as under her bed. They held the following conversation:

Lauren: My flashlight isn't reliable.

Dad: Why do you say that?

Lauren: Well, sometimes it just turns off for no reason. I have checked the batteries and I'm sure the bottom is on tight.

Dad: Maybe it's the bulb. Let's see if there is a spare in the closet.

Lauren: OK. I hadn't thought of that.

This conversation could easily have taken place between two adults.

New Essentials for Teaching Reading in PreK–2

Functions of Talk

Once these language skills develop, children talk for many purposes and in many ways. Michael Halliday (1975, pp. 19–21) defines the seven functions of language, outlined in Figure 1.1.

Language not only serves many functions, but circumstances often dictate what we really mean and what answer is appropriate. For example, when we pass an acquaintance on the street, we often ask, "How are you?" The expected answer is "Fine." We don't expect or want an elaborate discussion of how the acquaintance really is. When we meet with a good friend and ask the same question, we are greeted with the details of health, frustrations, and family events. We expect and get very different responses to the same question. Talk is not just about learning to speak; it also entails learning the appropriate speech for the circumstances.

Due to the complexities and subtleties of talk, it is imperative that schools foster deeper understandings. Elementary schools can continue to expand the work of caregivers and preschool teachers by giving children many opportunities to talk about concepts and ideas, and to engage in verbal exchanges with other children and adults. *opportunities to talk*

Figure 1.1

Functions of Talk

1. **Instrumental:** language used to satisfy a need.
   EXAMPLE: "Ball, Mommy."

2. **Regulatory:** language used to control the behavior of others.
   EXAMPLE: "No nap now."

3. **Interactional:** language used to get along with others.
   EXAMPLE: "Play with me."

4. **Personal:** language used to tell about one's self.
   EXAMPLE: "I'm four now."

5. **Heuristic:** language used to learn about things.
   EXAMPLE: "Where did the sun go?"

6. **Imaginative:** language used to pretend or make believe.
   EXAMPLE: "I'm a kitty."

7. **Informative:** language used to inform others.
   EXAMPLE: "This card has to go with that card."

Adapted from Halliday, 1975.

What the Research Says About . . .

Talk and Instruction

Researchers, such as Gordon Wells (1986) and Courtney Cazden (1988), agree that when children enter school their opportunities for talk change and become limited. It has been said that when children start school, they enter a time of language deprivation. There are several reasons for this alarming change.

Before entering school, children hold conversations on any topic of interest to them. Topics arise spontaneously and children are free to jump from topic to topic. Parents engage in one-on-one exchanges with their children, answering questions, giving directions, and providing explanations.

Once children begin school, all of this changes. There are one or two adults in a classroom of 20 to 25 children. Teachers cannot spend large amounts of time in conversation with one child. In addition, there are schedule issues that limit spontaneity. Curriculum demands and the number of children limit discussion topics. While children initiate conversations at home, at school teachers control who talks, when they can talk, and what topic will be discussed. Although it is necessary that the talk to which children are accustomed at home change, talk as a tool for learning can continue in the elementary classroom.

Talking to Learn During Reading

Many primary teachers schedule read-aloud time daily. Rather than having a simple question-and-answer time at the end of the story, children could benefit from expressive engagement. The term *expressive engagement* includes several types of responses. In his research, Lawrence R. Sipe (2002) describes the responses listed in Figure 1.2. Expressive engagement requires children to become deeply involved with text. Jane Morse's first-grade class offers an example.

Figure 1.2

Expressive Engagement

1. **Dramatizing:** Young children often use physical movements during stories. They may imitate the Big Bad Wolf by showing their teeth and using their hands as claws.

2. **Talking back:** While listening to the story of Little Red Riding Hood, the children may talk to the story or characters. Young listeners may "tell" Red Riding Hood not to talk to the wolf.

3. **Critiquing or controlling:** Children sometimes change the story with what they consider to be a more reasonable action. For example, during a reading of The Three Little Pigs, the children may decide that the pigs should all have built sturdy houses of brick.

4. **Inserting:** Inserting themselves and/or their friends into the story is another way young children express themselves while listening to read-alouds. While listening to The Gingerbread Man, Jamie remarked that Katie really ate the gingerbread man because her last name is Fox.

5. **Taking over:** By taking over and manipulating the text for their own purposes, children use the text as a springboard for their own stories.

Adapted from Sipe, 2002.

New Essentials for Teaching Reading in PreK–2

Her students were listening to a read-aloud of *Night Tree* by Eve Bunting (Harcourt, 1994). The book tells of a family carrying a blanket into the woods on a December night. "Dad, wrap me in the blanket," whispered Tiffany as she listened to the story. On another page the story tells of the family sitting quietly, hoping deer will return to the area. Daniel began to call the deer as one would a dog, "Here, deer. Here, boy! I'll feed you." These children were so engaged, they had inserted themselves into the story.

When the children were shown an illustration of animals eating the fruit and popcorn the family had placed on the tree, several children began to dramatize the scene. One child dramatized the deer with its front paws up on the tree eating the fruit. Another child crawled on the floor pretending to eat the nuts and bread. When the text on the page was read aloud, several children began to "sing" in the voices of the animals and behave as the animals would.

This ability to engage with text on a deep and meaningful level will allow these children to fully comprehend the story. Jane encourages expressive engagement during read-alouds and often places extension activities in centers based on the children's responses to the stories.

Talking to Learn During Writing

In his book, *Language and Learning* (1970), James Britton tells us, "Writing floats on a sea of talk." This talk is not only between teacher and child, but also among children. It includes talk about the mechanics of writing and about thoughts and ideas. Children need to talk before, during, and after writing.

- **Before writing.** The talk before writing allows for the formation and refinement of ideas. Children may talk to a writing partner, and by doing so, clarify thoughts and form stories. When children have an opportunity to talk before writing, they turn to their notebooks and journals ready to get their story on paper.

- **During writing.** Writing conferences are a time for children and teachers to talk about what the child is writing and how to refine the writing. Conferences held during the formation of the piece help keep children focused and reduce the need for extensive revision. They help children clarify their writing and add more ideas. Carl Anderson (2000) tells us, "Conferences are not the icing on the cake. They are the cake."

- **After writing.** When young writers read their writing during share time, they are again afforded the opportunity to talk about what they have written. Their peers ask questions and make suggestions. Writers are expected to give thoughtful answers. Throughout writing time, children learn through talk.

Classroom Behavior

If children learn through talk, how can teachers support children's talk while maintaining a productive learning environment? Understanding that children are not misbehaving when they are dramatizing during read-aloud or taking over a story helps teachers better define unwanted behavior. It may also be useful to spend time teaching children about effective listening and speaking skills.

During read-aloud, for example, teachers worry that a student will derail the story with a long, often unrelated, tale. They fear that spontaneous comments will cause the lesson to dissolve into chaos. Many unwanted behaviors occur because children have not been taught productive speaking and listening skills. It may be well worth our time to offer children some guidelines. See Figure 1.3 for an example of one teacher's guidelines.

Show-and-tell is one technique teachers use to provide time during the school day for talk and conversations. Without guidelines, however, show-and-tell can become an unproductive activity. Young children often ramble in their telling, bring the same item to share with nothing new to say, or speak so softly that other children cannot hear them. Simple guidelines—such as preparing what to say in advance, choosing topics and items the audience is interested in, and speaking so that everyone can hear—will teach children speaking and listening skills that will be useful throughout their lives. Listeners also need to be taught what the expectations are for them.

Although it may take some time for young children to learn and practice productive speaking and listening skills, the time is well spent. Once children are able to carry on conversations and discussions, the opportunities to teach and learn through talk are endless.

Responsive Classroom

Figure 1.3

Our Guidelines for Talk

In our classroom, we will:

- not interrupt others.
- respect the thoughts and ideas of others.
- speak in a voice that's not too loud or too soft.
- listen and respond to a conversation partner.

practice productive speaking listening

Second-Language Learners

Traveling to non-English-speaking countries and trying to communicate in another language can be very frustrating. A trip to South Korea reminded Anna of what a challenge it can be to meet even your most basic needs if you do not know the language. Locating food, transportation, and bathrooms consumed a great deal of her time and energy. As an adult literate in another language, Anna was able to use phrase books, previous experiences with trains and buses, and map-reading skills to manage. And since Anna had chosen to travel, the excitement and sense of adventure kept her spirits high. The trip lasted only a few days, and Anna returned to the United States and was soon back in her comfort zone.

Now imagine being four, five, or even eight years old and being required to spend a large part of your day in a room where the other 20 or so people all speak a different language. Imagine that you have only taken the beginning steps into literacy in your native language, and that your experiences are limited and different. What would keep your spirits high in these circumstances? It is easy to understand why children placed in this situation usually remain silent for a period of time.

In the past, parents of second-language learners had been encouraged to speak English at home. Well-meaning teachers had suggested this approach thinking that children would learn English more quickly if it were the only language they heard. Researchers have learned that this approach may not yield the hoped-for success. Some parents speak limited English themselves and, therefore, cannot model fluent speech. In addition, research shows that children who continue to grow in sophistication in their first language are able to carry this sophistication into second-language learning (Tabors, 1997).

Learning a second language requires time and opportunity. Basic interpersonal communication skills can be learned in one to two years, but academic language can take from five to eight years for proficiency (Cummins, 1979). In classrooms, some second-language learners may appear fluent but struggle academically. Young children attempting to learn a second language will benefit from classrooms where talk is encouraged. They will hear English in a meaningful context, and language will often be associated with manipulatives. Many activities currently practiced in preschool through second grade will support second-language learners.

Second-language learners need not only adult models but also many opportunities to talk with their peers. A comfortable environment where they can take chances and make errors is vital. They will thrive in classrooms such as those described in chapters 6 through 9.

♦ ♦ ♦ Final Thoughts ♦ ♦ ♦

Talk allows teachers to understand the thinking processes of the children in their classrooms. Children who are not adept at reading and writing may be able to demonstrate understandings orally. Second-language learners gain a great deal by having many opportunities to listen to native speakers and to engage in conversations. Savvy teachers can use talk to support all learners in the classroom and to ensure understanding of content.

 The foundation for comprehending text is in oral language because language is how we make sense of our experience in the world. The next chapter is about comprehension—what it is and how you can help children extend their abilities to use oral language to comprehend the world into abilities to comprehend the text.

CHAPTER 2

Comprehension

The Research on Fostering Comprehending Processes

Reading words without understanding is a string of meaningless noise.

—Don Holdaway

Susan Lacy finished reading aloud *Scruffy: A Wolf Finds His Place in the Pack* by Jim Brandenburg (Walker, 1996). From the responses of her first graders she knew they identified and empathized with Scruffy, a low-status adolescent in an arctic wolf pack who fulfilled the important job of tending and teaching the pups while the adults went off to hunt. The children were brimming with many comments and questions, ripe for a literature conversation.

Susan: Today when you talk with your literature conversation partner about this book I'd like you to start off with "I wonder." Who could tell us one thing you wonder about this book so we can hear how "I wonder" will sound?

[Darnell's hand shoots up, but she can't wait to be called on.]

Darnell: Uh-huh! I wonder why the other wolves were so mean to Scruffy!

Susan: Oh, I wondered that myself! That is a good example of how "I wonder" will sound. Sierra, if you were Darnell's conversation partner, what would you say to Darnell?

Sierra: I think Scruffy is still just a kid so that's maybe why the other wolves boss him around.

Susan: So, you think he was being bossed around by the other wolves? Well, you and Darnell could have a good talk about your different ideas about Scruffy.

Susan then reviewed the procedures for how to talk about literature with a partner. The children had been having literature conversations since the beginning of the year, and now they were able to talk independently with a partner with only a little reminder and some monitoring.

Susan: If Sierra were Darnell's conversation partner, she and Darnell would keep talking about Darnell's "I wonder" until they had talked as much about it as they wanted. Then, it would be Sierra's turn to say something she wondered about.

This is how a conversation works; each person takes turns saying something he or she wonders about, and then the partners talk about it. And remember, for a good conversation, partners sit facing each other to show that they really care about and are paying attention to what the other is saying.

Okay, find your conversation partner, sit face-to-face on the rug, and have a good conversation about a special arctic wolf.

Overview of the Chapter

Through rich conversations, Susan Lacy's students learn how to question, predict, infer, determine important ideas, make connections, evaluate, and synthesize. These are the strategies that researchers have identified as key to higher levels of thinking and comprehending (Block & Pressley, 2003; Block, Gambrell, & Pressley, 2002; Duke & Pearson, 2002; Keene & Zimmerman, 1997; Pressley, 2000).

from read alouds

In this chapter we synthesize the research on comprehension and comprehension instruction that is most applicable in early literacy contexts, from preschool to second grade. First, we begin with a definition of comprehension and distinguish between *comprehension* and *comprehending*. This distinction is important. For years, educators thought "comprehension had to be 'caught, rather than taught'" (Pearson, Roehler, Dole, & Duffy, 1992, p. 146). That's because they viewed comprehension as a product—either you had it or you didn't. New research suggests that comprehension is the result of a reader's astute use of a network of overlapping and interdependent comprehending processes (Block & Pressley, 2003; Duffy, 2003; Kristo & Bamford, 2004; Pearson et al., 1992). And these processes can be taught (Cole, 2003, 2004; Duke & Pearson, 2002; Harvey & Goudvis, 2000; Keene & Zimmerman, 1997; McLaughlin, 2003; Owocki, 2003; Pressley, 2002).

Comprehension Defined

The act of comprehending is a complex and highly individual process. John Steinbeck once said, "A story has as many versions as it has readers. Everyone takes what he can from it and thus changes it to his own measure. Some pick out parts and reject the rest, some strain the story through their own mesh of prejudices, some paint it with their own delight. A story must have some point of contact with the reader to make him feel at home with it" (1961, p. XX). Even with a nonfiction text, the children in Susan Lacy's first-grade classroom have different things they wonder about. Each child brings different life experiences and a different purpose for reading to his or her interpretation of the nonfiction text.

Life experiences influence comprehension

The Reader, the Text, the Purpose

Today, it is generally understood that reading any printed text requires the orchestration of a variety of *comprehending processes, such as predicting, inferring, monitoring, and questioning* (Bamford & Kristo, 2003; Duke & Pearson, 2002; Irwin, 1991; Pressley, 2000; Stahl, 2004; Sweet & Snow, 2002). And these comprehending processes may vary depending on the type of text read and the purpose. For example, a reader may skim a newspaper article to locate specific information, reread a passage in a textbook to take notes on the main idea, or read "between the lines" to infer a character's motivations in a novel. As shown in Figure 2.1, researchers and theorists suggest that comprehension is affected by three factors. (See Irwin, 1991, and the RAND Reading Study Group, 2002, for a thorough review of these three factors.)

It turns out that comprehension is a lot more complicated than we thought. For example, you cannot say that a reader either "has" comprehension or doesn't. Instead, you have to qualify your statement by saying that *a particular* reader can comprehend a *particular* text or text type when it suits his or her purpose. That particular reader may not comprehend another text or text type, especially, if he or she is not motivated to tackle it. And the complications of defining comprehension continue.

Figure 2.1

Factors Affecting Comprehension

- The **reader** who brings to the comprehending his or her accumulated sociocultural expectations, abilities, knowledge of content and comprehending processes, motivation to read, and prior experiences.

- The type and format of the **text** to be comprehended, including any printed or electronic media.

- The **purpose** for reading—the activities and context in which the reading takes place that affect how motivated the reader is to read.

Adapted from RAND, 2002.

Comprehension Versus Comprehending

It is important to distinguish between *comprehension* and *comprehending*, because one comes before the other (Goodman & Goodman, 2004, p. 625). That is, comprehending leads to comprehension. The word *comprehension* suggests a product—either you understand the main point of a text or you don't. You might ask children questions at the end of a read-aloud or a guided reading lesson to evaluate how well they understood the main idea or the motivation of the characters. But this doesn't help children learn how to comprehend.

Comprehending is the active process leading to comprehension. It is a process of bringing what you already know into the text in order to interpret, infer, and understand. Knowing how to pick out important information from peripheral details in a text is part of the comprehending process. Comprehending is also the active process of following a sequence of events in a story or following the topics and subtopics in a nonfiction book. It is also stopping when something doesn't make sense and going back to figure out what went wrong with the comprehending. You have to teach children how to use comprehending processes to achieve comprehension. Louise Rosenblatt captured the essence of comprehending versus comprehension: "Meaning emerges as the reader carries on a give-and-take with the signs on the page. . . . The two-way, reciprocal relation explains why meaning is not 'in' the text or 'in' the reader. Both reader and text are essential to the transactional process of making meaning" (1995, p. 26).

Comprehending—active processing—is the goal during reading. The current definition of comprehension encompasses comprehending processes. Cathy Block and Michael Pressley suggest that comprehending processes "can be defined as a set of meaning-making skills, strategies, and thought processes that readers initiate at specific points in a text to understand, apply, and appreciate authors' writings" (2003, pp. 114–115).

What the Research Says About . . .

Comprehending Processes

Much of what we know about reading comprehension as a process and about effective reading comprehension instruction has been learned since 1975 (Duke & Pearson, 2002). The comprehension research has been grounded in studies of good readers, and now we know a great deal about what good readers do. They do not sit back and wait passively for meaning to come to them; they construct the meaning. As Figure 2.2 shows, researchers have identified the interactive network of comprehending processes that good readers of fiction and nonfiction use (Block & Pressley, 2003; Duffy, 2003; Kristo & Bamford, 2004; Pearson et al., 1992).

This research asks us to rethink traditional notions of a tightly knit sequence of "comprehension skills" in a curriculum scope and sequence chart. Rather, comprehension is the result of interactive and overlapping comprehending processes that form a network of thinking/reading strategies. Pearson et al. (1992) synthesized the emerging research on comprehension for the second edition of the International Reading Association publication *What Research Has to Say About Reading Instruction*. They turned comprehension instruction in a new direction:

Comprehending Processes

- **Activating background knowledge.** Good readers know how to use what they've already learned about the world, about how people behave, and about how books work; they activate this knowledge to make sense from life in general and from books. This process is really a precursor to all the other comprehending processes, because you can't predict, infer, or imagine without using background knowledge. Many poor readers do not realize that reading is as much about what you already know as it is about what the text is saying (Paris & Lindauer, 1976).

- **Predicting.** Good readers anticipate that a text is going to make sense. They predict what they think is going to happen and revise their predictions as they gather more information during reading.

- **Using different comprehending processes on different types of text.** When reading fiction, good readers attend to the plot, the sequence of events, the characters, and the setting. They usually read from beginning to end. When reading nonfiction, good readers attend to graphic organizers (e.g., table of contents, headings, index) and how the information is organized (e.g., compare-contrast, cause-effect, chronological). They might not read from beginning to end but rather might pick and choose the most important sections for the information they need.

- **Making connections.** Good readers follow an author's train of thought, making connections *within* the text between details and main ideas. Good readers also make connections *between* texts (e.g., Hey! There was a cat like this in the last book I read), and they make connections between the text and themselves (e.g., The girl in the story is a lot like me).

- **Imagining.** Good readers respond to the descriptive text they read. They see, hear, smell, taste, and even feel what is happening in the text. Some who write about comprehension have called this "visualizing" (e.g., Keene & Zimmerman, 1997), but we think the term *imagining* more aptly captures the full range of senses a reader activates to comprehend.

- **Inferring.** Inferring is the ability to read between the lines or to get the meaning an author implies but does not state directly. However, it is not wild guessing. Inferring is a thoughtful and systematic process of using the clues an author supplies combined with a reader's own background knowledge.

New Essentials for Teaching Reading in PreK–2

- **Monitoring, questioning, and repairing.** Comprehending requires that the reader figuratively "listen" to the text as it is unfolding to make sure it makes sense and sounds right. For example, if a good reader detects a mismatch between predictions and how the text is actually unfolding, he or she begins searching for a way to reconcile the mismatch by asking questions of the author (e.g., What is the author saying here?), the text (e.g., Why isn't the character doing something else?), and self (e.g., Did I read something incorrectly?). Then, good readers repair what doesn't make sense or sound right by answering the question and fixing it. A child's self-corrections when reading text orally are evidence of this monitor-question-repair cycle, and you can capture it on running records (Clay, 2000).

- **Distinguishing important ideas from less important ones.** Good readers can separate the wheat from the chaff in a text. In traditional comprehension research and instruction, this is often referred to as the main idea, theme, thesis, or topic of a text. But note that these all refer to the *product* of comprehending. Students need to learn the *process* of determining what is central to the text and what is extraneous. We have often noticed undergraduates who underline or highlight almost the whole textbook in our classes and wonder if we should be teaching the critical comprehending process of distinguishing important ideas.

- **Summarizing.** Good readers can create a brief retelling of an entire text, and the emphasis is on *brief*. Poor readers often retell many details in a lengthy narrative. Clearly, summarizing is closely related to distinguishing important ideas.

- **Evaluating.** Good readers go beyond the message and make judgments about what the author is saying. For example, even young children can learn how to evaluate whether a book is fiction or nonfiction and judge how accurate the information in a nonfiction text might be. Evaluating is a particularly important process in today's "information age." Infomercials are cleverly designed, so it is hard to tell what is fact and what is advertising.

- **Synthesizing.** Good readers can bring together information from a variety of sources to create a single understanding. This is what students are required to do when they bring together information from across several texts to do a research report. But even young children can learn to synthesize information within a single text.

We really do expect *all* readers of *all* ages to engage in *all* of these strategies at some level of sophistication. We really are arguing that there are no first-grade skills, third-grade skills, sixth-grade skills, and so on. Readers of all ages should engage in these strategies; with age and experience, they get better and are able to apply them to a wider range of texts, tasks, and situations. But, these strategies are as important for the novice as they are for the expert. Granted, first graders may not ask sophisticated questions, but they can ask something, and what they ask is likely to be important to them. (pp. 169–170)

first graders / novices

What these researchers are suggesting is that learning comprehending processes is like learning many skilled human actions (e.g., riding a bike, playing the piano, building a house). The more the interacting processes are used and practiced on increasingly difficult tasks, the greater the expertise becomes.

practice

This view of reading comprehension contrasts sharply with traditional views of reading instruction that focused efforts on decoding in the preK–2 years and then turned to comprehension in the later grades. And then, comprehension instruction consisted of assigning reading and requiring students to fill out grade-level workbook exercises assessing comprehension "skills" such as identifying the main idea. We agree with Pearson et. al (1992) that the interactive network of comprehending processes should constitute the curriculum for reading comprehension instruction in every grade.

What the Research Says About . . .
Teaching Comprehending Processes

Given knowledge about what good readers do when they read, researchers and educators have asked, Can we teach students to do what good readers do? A large volume of work indicates that we can help students acquire the strategies and processes used by good readers. There is a wide range of instructional methods that work (Duke & Pearson, 2002), and there are several new books by practitioners that demonstrate how to put comprehension research and theory into practice (e.g., Block, Rodgers, & Johnson, 2004; Cole, 2003; Harvey & Goudvis, 2000; Kristo & Bamford, 2004; McLaughlin, 2003; Owocki, 2003). In general, effective comprehension instruction involves both explicit instruction in specific comprehension strategies and lots of time for children to engage in reading, writing, and discussion of text. In other words, comprehension instruction is not just one method, but a collection of practices across the school day that foster meaning-making processes.

Our focus here is on a collection of instructional practices most appropriate for preschool to second-grade contexts. First, we address some general features of the classroom context for effective comprehension instruction. Then, because talk is so critical to young children's learning, we address the role of talk in comprehension instruction. We cover two specific practices for comprehension instruction that have strong backing in the research and can be applied effectively in early literacy contexts.

Classroom Context for Effective Comprehension Instruction

It is not enough just to offer good comprehension instruction. Outlined briefly here are several features critical for comprehension instruction to take hold and flourish. You will see them in action in Part II.

- **Time spent reading.** All the instruction in the world will not make up for a lack of experience actually reading and applying strategies and skills taught. Even very young children who read very simple texts need an opportunity to independently reread those texts every day. For the youngest readers, rereading familiar text not only reinforces comprehending and decoding processes but also fosters fluency, a topic we cover in Chapter 4. For more experienced readers in early literacy classrooms, time spent reading new text in preparation for a guided discussion is a powerful tool for fostering comprehension.

- **Experience with a range of text genres.** Spoken language is different in many ways from written language (Garton & Pratt, 1998; Moats, 2000). Young readers need an opportunity to develop an ear for the language and literary structures they will eventually read themselves. Therefore, teachers need carefully chosen and wide read-aloud and shared-reading libraries, including fiction and nonfiction genres.

- **Experience hearing and reading texts for authentic purposes.** To truly understand why people read, young readers need opportunities to hear and read texts for authentic purposes. Classrooms rich in content area investigations and integrated, thematic instruction provide opportunities for young children to read for real purposes.

- **Vocabulary and concept development.** Text comprehension depends to a large extent on knowledge of vocabulary. You can create a classroom context that arouses children's interest in and awareness of words by talking about words and their connections and by using word walls, word collections, and wordplay. See Chapter 3 for a more thorough discussion of the research relating to vocabulary and comprehension.

- **Opportunities to build reading fluency.** The foundation for comprehension is fast, accurate reading to maintain meaning over long stretches of text. You can foster the foundation for comprehension through activities that build reading fluency. See Chapter 4 for a thorough discussion of fluency research and classroom practice.

- **Opportunities to write texts for others to comprehend.** Writing their own messages for other people to read makes it clear to young children as nothing else does that written words have a purpose. Classroom contexts for young readers should emphasize connections between reading and writing and develop young readers' abilities to write like a reader and read like a writer.

- **A comprehensive classroom literacy program to accommodate students of diverse backgrounds.** A growing body of research points to the effectiveness of student access to a continuum of teacher-supported (e.g., shared and guided) and independent reading opportunities, particularly as classrooms fill with students of more diverse backgrounds. (See Au, 2002, for a review of the research on effective instruction for students of diverse backgrounds.) Classrooms that accommodate students of diverse backgrounds should provide motivation for reading and writing through content area investigations and integrated instruction. They also should use a variety of supportive instructional practices, such as shared and guided reading and literature discussion groups. And finally, classrooms that accommodate diverse learners should provide for differences in cultural experiences through use of a range of multicultural literature.

Teaching comprehending processes encompasses much more than knowing how to use a particular teaching method. It influences

- ◆ how you manage classroom time,
- ◆ the books you choose to read to or share with children,
- ◆ the experiences you provide in content area inquiries,
- ◆ the instructional methods you use to support and scaffold children's reading.

Now, we turn to the second aspect we feel is critical to teaching comprehending processes in early literacy contexts: talk.

The Role of Talk in Teaching and Learning Comprehending Processes

As adults, we talk to others about interesting materials we have read—such as newspaper articles and novels. With our colleagues we discuss professional readings. Our talk helps us understand, learn different perspectives, and clarify our own thinking. The same holds true for the children we teach. The talk to foster comprehending processes may be either informal through teacher think-alouds (Duke & Pearson, 2002; Wilhelm, 2001) or more formal through explicit teaching (Duke & Pearson, 2002; Pressley, 2002). Thoughtful, focused talk—teacher-to-students and student-to-student— permeates a classroom in which comprehending processes can take hold and flourish. Let's look at two research-based instructional practices that use talk to foster comprehending processes.

Think-Aloud

As its name implies, think-aloud instruction involves making one's thoughts audible, and usually, public. In the case of reading, it means saying what you are thinking while you are reading. A teacher think-aloud is typically considered a form of teacher modeling (Duke & Pearson, 2002; Wilhelm, 2001). When thinking aloud, teachers demonstrate effective comprehending processes and show when and where to apply them. For example, when Kelly Berube read *Tops & Bottoms* by Janet Stevens (Harcourt, 1995) to her first graders, she often stopped and wondered aloud like this: "I wonder how he'll trick the bear *this* time. If the bear gets both the tops *and* the bottoms of the plant, what will be left for the hare? Let's keep going to find out." She modeled how a reader maintains comprehending throughout a story by wondering and then reading to find out.

You can use think-aloud to model comprehending processes during read-alouds, shared reading, or guided reading. Teacher modeling through think-aloud is most effective when it is explicit, leaving the student to intuit or infer little about the comprehending process being modeled and its application (Duke & Pearson, 2002).

Instruction that includes having students think aloud themselves also has proven effective at improving comprehension of text. (For a review of that research, see Kucan & Beck, 1997.) Thinking aloud provides young children with an opportunity to practice in a concrete way the conversations readers have with themselves as they read, think about, and comprehend a text. You can guide young children in thinking aloud by stopping during a read-aloud or shared reading and asking students to talk about what they are thinking. You would do this only after you had modeled thinking aloud yourself. For example, after modeling how she was wondering what the hare would plant next in *Tops & Bottoms*, Kelly might stop and ask students to say aloud what they were thinking about the characters or their actions.

A Model of Comprehension Instruction

Nell Duke and P. David Pearson (2002) suggest an instructional model for teaching comprehension that has five components. The components describe a rough scaffold that provides increasingly less support for readers as they learn to take over the comprehending processes themselves. Figure 2.3 outlines their model and gives examples of how the components might be applied in a second-grade guided reading group that is learning how to apply the comprehending process of integrating prior knowledge. In this example, these more experienced readers are reading a chapter book mystery involving some children who are camping, and the teacher knows the children have background knowledge about camping.

All five components occur during the same lesson, but they don't always have to. For example, in a kindergarten classroom or early in the year in first grade you might spend most of the time modeling (component 2) different comprehension strategies using think-aloud during read-alouds. Then, during that same span of time, you might provide collaborative use of the strategies (component 3) or guided practice (component 4) during shared-reading activities. You might not get to component 5, independent use of the strategy, until children are ready to read books on their own in guided-reading groups. In other words, these five components do not have to be implemented in a lockstep manner. Instead, you could think of this as an *apprenticeship model* (Dorn, French, & Jones, 1998; Kristo & Bamford, 2004). The components provide increasingly less support from the teacher as young readers develop more competence with reading.

We suggest that *all* students be introduced to comprehending processes first through think-alouds during read-aloud or shared-reading sessions. Then, more experienced readers, such as first and second graders at the transitional phase of reading (i.e., instructional text levels 14–28), can be taught to apply comprehending processes during guided reading.

If a preK–2 team of teachers has agreed on and then work together to teach a curriculum of comprehending processes, by the time students reach

Figure 2.3

Comprehension Instruction: Second-Grade Guided Reading Group

1. **An explicit description of the strategy and when and how it should be used.** "Good readers use their prior knowledge—what they already know—to help them understand. Often, all the information you need to understand is not in the book; you have to use what you already know and the author's hints to understand. For example . . ."

2. **Teacher and/or student modeling of the strategy in action.** "I am going to use what's in my head already to figure out what time of day it is in the story. The author writes, 'The setting sun glinted on the water.' I know that if the sun is setting, it must be late afternoon or early evening, but the author never says that exactly. I had to use what was in my head to understand that it was late afternoon or early evening."

3. **Collaborative use of the strategy in action.** "Let's all read the next page silently. See if you can use what is in your head to figure out what the two boys are doing. . . . Okay, let's hear what you think the two boys are doing (they are setting up a campsite) and what you used in your head to figure this out (they are pitching a tent, building a fire, getting water from the lake)."

4. **Guided practice using the strategy with gradual release of responsibility.** "Now, read the next three pages to yourself. See if you can tell how the boys are feeling. Be ready to tell us what information you used from your head that helped you know." Later on . . .

   "As you are reading the rest of the story, notice how you use what is in your head and the author's hints, along with the author's words, to really understand. Mark sections of the book with a sticky note, and when we meet later today I'll ask you to tell us about those places where you used your head and the author's words to understand."

5. **Independent use of the strategy.** "As you are reading in preparation for your book discussion group, remember to use what is in your head, hints the author gives, and what the author actually says to understand."

Adapted from Duke & Pearson, 2002.

first and second grade, they would already recognize and use them. In preschool and kindergarten, students would be introduced to these processes as listeners through teacher think-alouds during read-alouds and shared reading of a wide variety of genres. In first and second grade, these learners would apply these processes as they listened to more-complex texts, as they did think-alouds themselves, and as they read texts on their own in guided reading groups and literature discussion groups.

Pre K – K
read alouds
shared reading

♦ ♦ ♦ Final Thoughts ♦ ♦ ♦

To really understand what they read, good readers access background knowledge, make predictions, imagine, infer, question and monitor, and make connections, all together, on the run, as they are reading. Therefore, while it makes sense to teach comprehending processes one at a time, it also makes sense to make sure that students know they need to connect and integrate them.

While comprehending processes are critical variables, students need to learn much more in order to develop effective meaning-making systems. Knowing lots of words, and knowing connections *between* words, helps students comprehend text more effectively. Therefore, we turn to vocabulary learning and teaching next, in Chapter 3.

Vocabulary

The Research on Fostering Vocabulary Development

As children are developing their reading and writing competence, we need to take advantage of their listening and speaking competencies to enhance their vocabulary development. We certainly must not hold back adding vocabulary to children's repertoires until their word recognition becomes adequate. Thus a major source for identifying interesting words are the delightful trade books that are read to children.

—Beck, McKeown, and Kucan

trade books

The annual Fourth of July parade was so crowded that Carol's family could hardly move or see much of the parade. Her young son, Jason, listened to his parents complaining about how crowded it was. Later that week, while on a trip to the grocery store, Carol and Jason saw a man walking along the sidewalk, tipping his head and squinting hard to see through the blinding morning sun. Jason looked up and declared, "Mommy! That man is crowded!" To Carol's surprise, Jason had astutely noted that the man was squinting so hard that the features on his face were all crowded together.

Like many novice language users, Jason was trying out new learning but applying it in a somewhat unconventional way. Most seasoned language users would not refer to a person's face as "crowded." Jason will need several more experiences with the concept of *crowded* to be able to use it in a conventional manner. He will need experiences with the feeling of *crowded*, explicit explanations for the meaning of *crowded*, and opportunities to see when *crowded* applies and when it does not.

Overview of the Chapter

Much vocabulary learning for young children is implicit, learned in the context of talk around joint activities. However, vocabulary researchers (e.g., Beck, McKeown, & Kucan, 2002) argue that implicit learning from context is not enough to develop in-depth knowledge of word meaning. Many students need explicit and robust instruction about the meaning of words, and repeated encounters with the same words, to really learn all the nuances related to knowing words completely. In this chapter we summarize research on vocabulary development and the implications for research-based vocabulary instruction.

What the Research Says About . . .
Vocabulary Development

What does it mean to know a word? Knowing a word is not an all-or-nothing proposition. For example, you may have a superficial grasp of the meaning of a word but not be able to use the word accurately in new contexts. First, we look at what it means to know a word. Then we look at two other areas of research that have implications in early literacy contexts. The first is the research on vocabulary learning in children affected by poverty. The second is the research connecting reading comprehension and vocabulary knowledge.

What It Means to Know a Word

Researchers have identified four stages in word learning as well as several important dimensions to knowing a word: knowing words have multiple meanings and knowing the ways in which words are interrelated.

Four Stages of Word Learning. Dale (1965) suggested that word learning falls into four stages:

1. You've never heard the word before.
2. You've heard the word, but you don't know what it means.
3. You recognize and can use the word in a familiar context but not in new contexts.
4. You know the word well and can use it in many contexts.

Another way to think about word learning is that it may fall along a continuum: from no knowledge of a word at one end to a rich, multidimensional understanding of a word at the other end, including understanding the word's relationship to other words and its extension to metaphorical uses, such as understanding what it means when someone "washes his hands of something."

Knowing Words Have Multiple Meanings. Knowing a word in-depth involves recognizing that words can have multiple meanings. For example, Jason will learn that *wash* can refer to what he does in the morning with his washcloth as well as to the pile of dirty clothes in the laundry room. He will also learn that he can wash his face, wash cars, wash clothes, and wash the dog. In addition, knowing a word really well means being able to understand analogy and wordplay related to it. For example, in the book for early readers *Mrs. Wishy-Washy* by Joy Cowley (Philomel Books, 1990), a frustrated farm wife tries to keep some very naughty animals clean. Knowing the word *wash* includes being able to appreciate the refrain "wishy-washy, wishy-washy" as an industrious Mrs. Wishy-Washy scrubs each muddy animal in the tub.

Knowing How Words Are Interrelated. Vocabulary learners also have to learn the many ways in which meanings of words are interrelated. For example, how well Jason understands the meaning of *crowded* will be linked to his knowledge of other words describing spatial relationships (e.g., a street congested with traffic or a room crammed with too much furniture). Jason's knowledge of *crowded* will also be affected by his knowledge of words such as *empty*, *deserted*, and *spacious*. The more Jason learns about other words describing spatial relationships, the deeper he will understand the word *crowded* and how it applies to groups of too many people or too much furniture but not to faces squinting in the sun. So knowing a word well also means understanding homonyms, homographs, antonyms, and synonyms that might be related to it.

Children Affected by Poverty

The typical middle-class child learns approximately 3,000 to 4,000 words each year, accumulating a reading vocabulary of approximately 25,000 words by the end of elementary school and approximately 50,000 words by the end of high school (Nagy & Anderson, 1984; White, Graves, & Slater, 1990). Research indicates that growing up in poverty can significantly restrict the academic vocabulary children learn before beginning school, and it can make attaining an adequate academic vocabulary a challenging task (Hart & Risley, 1995; White, 1990).

Life and literacy experiences offer preschool children opportunities to develop vocabulary knowledge. Children from poor homes are less likely than their more affluent classmates to have experienced visits to the zoo or vacations at the beach. Such activities carry their own unique vocabulary and lead to conversations that develop this vocabulary in context.

In addition to life experiences, children growing up in poverty are less likely to have the same literacy experiences as middle-class children. Adams (1991) estimates that by the time many middle-class children reach first grade they may have had between 1,000 and 1,700 hours of storybook reading, including many opportunities for talk and interaction around the books. They may have spent more than 1,000 hours watching and interacting with parents around *Sesame Street*. And they may have spent at least as many hours playing with magnetic letters on the refrigerator, writing, participating in reading/writing/language activities in preschool, and playing word and language games in the car and on the computer with family and friends. In contrast, some children living in poverty were found to have as little as 25 hours of storybook experience and no more than 200 hours of general experience with the form and function of print (Adams, 1990; Clay, 1976; Feitelson & Goldstein, 1986; Heath, 1983).

Children growing up in poverty, whether urban or rural dwellers, have a lot of school-related vocabulary learning to do to catch up to their more advantaged peers. In order to develop an adequate school-related vocabulary, some students may need many more opportunities to engage in vocabulary study early in preschool and kindergarten.

Connecting Reading Comprehension and Vocabulary Knowledge

Reading is critical for success in all academic subjects and in the world beyond school. Therefore, it is important to note the connection between vocabulary and reading comprehension, which is supported by a large body of research (Nagy, 1988). Readers cannot understand much of what they read without knowing what most of the words mean. Anderson and Freebody (1981) found that a reader's general vocabulary knowledge is the single best predictor of how well a reader can understand. However, research also suggests that reading *influences* vocabulary. Baker, Simmons, and Kameenui (1995) found that the relationship between reading comprehension and vocabulary knowledge is strong, but not well understood. There is evidence that the relationship is reciprocal. In other words, how well you read influences how well you learn vocabulary; in turn, how well you understand vocabulary influences how well you comprehend.

This is a bit like the chicken-and-egg debate. Which comes first, the vocabulary or the reading? At least one researcher, Nagy (1988), believes that reading comes first. He declared, "What is needed to produce vocabulary growth is not more vocabulary instruction, but more reading" (p. 3). This presents a dilemma for vocabulary development in preK–2; the children don't yet read much on their own, and by design, to facilitate learning how to read, the books young children can read are very simple, with familiar words and known concepts. Beck et al. (2002) suggest, therefore, that the best sources for vocabulary instruction are the books teachers read to children. High-quality read-aloud texts contain rich, sophisticated language.

Read alouds to facilitate vocabulary learning

We agree but would also add that there are many opportunities for vocabulary development during the school day. As we outlined in Chapter 1, talk around content area activities, read-alouds, and shared reading is a major vehicle for vocabulary development in young children.

talk

The summary of research related to vocabulary instruction that follows not only provides support for why you should teach vocabulary in the early grades but also explains what it means for children to really know a word.

Vocabulary Instruction

Vocabulary can be a factor in school achievement in general, and comprehension in particular. This makes vocabulary instruction critical not only for disadvantaged students but for all students. In this section, we'll look at four key questions that arise as we consider vocabulary instruction and young children.

1) How Should Concepts and Vocabulary Be Taught?

As classrooms become increasingly diverse, it is important to consider all learners when planning vocabulary instruction. Graves and Graves (1994) suggest that there is a difference between teaching vocabulary and teaching concepts. For example, second-language learners come to our classrooms with many concepts in their first language (e.g., *table*, *hot*, or *run*) that have been developed through life experiences. These children are then taught the English vocabulary for the concepts. However, young children in any culture have to learn both the concepts and the vocabulary. In the case of Jason, he is learning both the concept for *crowded* and the vocabulary for naming it. Researchers suggest that concept-based vocabulary instruction has the most lasting impact on student learning (Allen, 1999; Thompkins & Blanchfield, 2004).

Concepts can be connected with vocabulary development during instruction in a variety of ways:

♦ **Teach new concepts and new vocabulary together.** For example, Jason learns both the concept and the word for *crowded*.

♦ **Teach new words for existing concepts.** For example, Jason learns the new words *launder, cleanse,* and *bathe* and relates them to the known word *wash.*

♦ **Teach so that students relate known words to new concepts.** For example, Jason knows what a *cup* for milk is and learns the new concept of *cupping* his hands to drink water or to hoist a friend over a fence.

♦ **Teach so that students relate known words to known concepts.** For example, Jason learns that *dog* can refer not only to the family pet but also to a family of wild animals.

Throughout this book, teaching vocabulary will refer to both the teaching of concepts and the vocabulary for naming the concept.

2) How Should Words Be Selected?

To get an estimate of the kinds of words that need instruction, Beck et al. (2002) identified three categories, or tiers, of words. (See Figure 3.1.) The first tier comprises the most basic words you would encounter in everyday life: *clock*, *baby*, *happy*, *walk*. Words in Tier One rarely need instructional attention to their meanings in school. However, these words are likely to be the ones you teach as sight words because they are the most frequently used words in the English language. Rapid recognition of Tier One words will make reading more fluent; the ability to write these words quickly will make writing more fluent. Tier One words will be discussed in greater depth in Chapter 4, on fluency.

At the other end of the continuum are Tier Three words. Words in this category are rarely used, except in specific, content area contexts. *Isotope*, *lathe*, *peninsula*, and *refinery* are examples of Tier Three words. They are best taught within context, as needed, to comprehend the subject matter, rather than in a general vocabulary development program. That is, you will teach Tier Three words, but only in the content area studies appropriate to young children in preschool through grade two.

Tier Two words are not used as frequently as Tier One words, but they are of high utility for understanding concepts in more-complex books and language usage. Tier Two includes words such as *coincide*, *absurd*, *industrious*, and *fortunate*. Words such as these describe abstract concepts as opposed to concrete objects or actions, like *baby*, *clock*, and *cry*, which are Tier One words. Therefore, Tier Two words play a large role in shaping a broad, mature vocabulary, and they can have a powerful impact on verbal functioning. Consequently, most vocabulary instruction should be focused on Tier Two words.

Beck et al. (2002) suggest that there are no hard-and-fast rules regarding words to teach in preschool, kindergarten, and first and second grades. Simply select words from books you read aloud or share with children. Aim for Tier Two words that are not too difficult to explain to young children. For example, *accidental*, *drowsy*, and *envious* are easy to explain because most youngsters already have concepts for these words: *accidental* means by mistake; *drowsy* means sleepy; *envious* means desirous of something someone else has.

Here's a paragraph from *Princess Furball* by Charlotte Huck (Green-

> ### Figure 3.1
>
> ### Tiers of Words for Vocabulary Instruction
>
> **Tier One:** Basic, everyday words that require little instruction.
>
> **Tier Two:** Less common, more abstract words that play a large role in shaping a mature vocabulary.
>
> **Tier Three:** Least common words related to specific content areas.
>
> Adapted from Beck, McKeown, & Kucan, 2002.

willow, 1989). See if you can identify Tier Two words you might use for vocabulary development in kindergarten or first grade.

The princess was horrified when she heard what her father had done, and begged him to change his mind. But her father was determined to carry out his bargain. The princess then thought of a clever plan. "Father," she said, "before I marry I must have three bridal gifts—One dress as golden as the sun, another as silvery as the moon, and a third as glittering as the stars. In addition, I shall need a coat made of a thousand different kinds of fur, one piece from every animal in our kingdom." (unpaged)

Figure 3.2

Making Word Choices in Vocabulary Instruction: Questions to Consider

- How generally useful is the word? Is it a word that students are likely to meet often in other texts? Will it be of use to students in describing their own experiences?

- How does the word relate to other words, to ideas that students know or have been learning? Does it directly relate to some topic of study in the classroom? Or might it add a dimension to ideas that have been developed?

- What does the word bring to the text or situation? What role does the word play in communicating the meaning of the context in which it is used?

Adapted from Beck, McKeown, & Kucan, 2002.

What Tier Two words would you pick? We chose *horrified*, *determined*, and *clever*. While there are lots of interesting words in this passage, these three words have high utility for mature language use and are easy to explain to young children. Figure 3.2 lists questions Beck et al. (2002) suggest teachers keep in mind while making word choices for vocabulary instruction. There is no formula for selecting grade-appropriate words for vocabulary instruction. As long as a word can be explained in terms young children can understand, it is an appropriate word to teach (Beck et al.).

3) How Many Words Should Be Taught Each Year?

Beck et al. (2002) say there is no way to know for sure how many words should be taught each year. However, their research indicates that instruction in about 400 words during the school year resulted in improvements in students' word knowledge and reading comprehension. While this may seem unrealistic, consider that this is only about ten words a week in a typical 40-week United States school year, or two to three words per day.

Vocabulary instruction for young children often happens through natural talk about a topic. However, you have to be conscious about noticing Tier Two words as they come up and initiating talk about the words. Classrooms

be conscious of Tier Two words in talk

New Essentials for Teaching Reading in PreK–2

rich in reading, writing, and talking provide multiple opportunities for making appropriate word choices and increasing vocabulary learning.

4) What Are the Most Effective Teaching Strategies?

Graves and Watts-Taffe (2002, pp. 142–143) suggest a four-part research-based approach to vocabulary development: wide reading, teaching individual words, teaching word learning strategies, and fostering word consciousness. This approach offers a framework for teacher decision making that supports effective vocabulary instruction. It also fits easily into early literacy instructional contexts.

vocabulary development

Four-Part Research-Based Approach to Vocabulary Development

Part 1: Wide Reading. Both theory (Sternberg, 1987) and recent research confirm that many words are learned in the context of reading (Nagy, Herman, & Anderson, 1985). Thus, one way to help students increase their vocabularies is to increase the amount of reading they do (Anderson, 1996; Anderson & Nagy, 1992; Nagy, 1988; S. A. Stahl, 1998). While young children may not read widely themselves, teachers can read to young children from a wide variety of high-quality fiction and nonfiction books. They can also share reading with young children from a growing number of high-quality fiction and nonfiction big books (see Moore, 2003, for a review of nonfiction big books for emergent, early, and transitional readers).

The implication here is that you need lots of good books for read-alouds and shared reading in early literacy contexts. Books and the decisions you make about using them to teach words are your vocabulary program—you don't need to buy a commercial one. Instead, you can use vocabulary instruction as a rationale for building your classroom library of children's literature and big books.

build classroom library

Part 2: Teaching Individual Words. Researchers caution that context alone is insufficient and inadequate to foster robust vocabulary development for some children (see Beck et al., 2002, for a review of the limitations of context in vocabulary learning). Therefore, effective, research-based vocabulary development must also include teaching individual words. As suggested earlier, Tier Two words can be taught in the context of read-aloud and shared reading. Teaching about two or three individual words a day seems to be adequate for substantially increasing children's vocabulary development. (In Part II of this book, instructional strategies will be discussed in depth.)

Many recent books and articles about vocabulary development suggest research-based methods for teaching individual words (Allen, 1999; Beck et al., 2002; Blachowicz & Fisher, 2002; Duffy, 2003; Thompkins & Blanch-field, 2004). The six-step sequence suggested by Beck et al. is particularly useful while teaching Tier Two vocabulary, and Tier Three vocabulary from content area studies or nonfiction literature. Figure 3.3 shows the six-step sequence for teaching the word *reluctant*, which was drawn from *A Pocket for Corduroy* by Don Freeman (Viking, 1978), a story about a teddy bear named Corduroy, who spends the night at a Laundromat.

Part 3: Teaching Word-Learning Strategies. In order to help students increase their vocabularies, it is important to explicitly teach word-learning strategies. For example, the use of context to predict the meaning of a word is most appropriate and useful for young children. This strategy is supported by research (Fukkink & de Glopper, 1998; Graves, 2000; Kuhn & Stahl, 1998; Stahl, 1998; Sternberg, 1987) and is an important part of a comprehensive focus on vocabulary instruction. The strategy can easily be taught during read-alouds and shared reading, with the teacher modeling the thinking a reader uses to figure out the meaning of an unknown word using the context. (See Part II of this book for more classroom examples of this strategy.)

use context

Figure 3.3

Six-Step Sequence for Teaching Tier Two Vocabulary

1. **Contextualize the word for its role in the story.** Teacher: "In the story, Lisa was *reluctant* to leave the Laundromat without Corduroy."

2. **Ask the students to repeat the word so that they can create a phonological representation of it.** Teacher: "Say the word *reluctant* with me."

3. **Explain the meaning of the word.** Teacher: "*Reluctant* means you are not sure you want to do something."

4. **Provide examples in contexts other than the one used in the story.** Teacher: "Someone might be reluctant to eat a food that they never had before, or someone might be reluctant to ride a roller coaster because it looks scary."

5. **Encourage students to interact with examples or provide their own examples.** Teacher: "Tell about something you would be reluctant to do. Try to use *reluctant* when you tell about it. You could start by saying, I would be reluctant to _____."

6. **Have students say the word again to reinforce its phonological representation.** Teacher: "What's the word we've been talking about?"

Adapted from Beck, McKeown, & Kucan, 2002.

New Essentials for Teaching Reading in PreK–2

Part 4: Fostering Word Consciousness.
Simply put, word consciousness is an aware-ness of and interest in words. While there are some specific teaching strategies to fos-ter it, word consciousness is as much about an attitude as it is about explicit instruction. Word consciousness is often fostered through implicit, rather than explicit, methods. For example, you can model an awareness of and interest in words by encouraging word collections such as word walls related to specific topics.

Janet Allen (1999), who writes about teaching vocabulary to older students, shared a unique way to build word con-sciousness by collecting words in jars, either real jars or jar-shaped drawings on the bulletin board. Allen and her students choose words to put in their jars that tickle the ears, warm the heart, make them wonder, make them feel smart, and so on. The possibilities are endless. The main idea is to collect words!

Four-Part Research-Based Approach to Vocabulary Instruction: A Quick Guide

Part 1: Wide Reading. Choose books for read-aloud and shared reading from a wide variety of high-quality children's literature and big books.

Part 2: Teaching Individual Words. Teach two or three individual words each day. Follow a sequence such as the following: 1) Remind stu-dents of the context for the word in the book, 2) ask students to say the word aloud, 3) explain the meaning of the word, 4) provide examples of other contexts in which the word might be used, 5) ask students to use the word themselves, and 6) ask students to say the word again.

Part 3: Teaching Word-Learning Strategies. Explicitly teach the children specific strategies to figure out the meaning of new words.

Part 4: Fostering Word Consciousness. Create a classroom context in which awareness of and interest in words are aroused.

Adapted from Graves & Watts-Taffe, 2002.

Other Considerations for a Research-Based Vocabulary Program

In addition to Graves & Watts-Taffe's four-part approach (summarized in Figure 3.4), there are two additional areas to consider in a research-based vocabulary program: making connections between words and maintaining vocabulary knowledge.

Making Connections Between Words. It is not enough to focus simply on teaching and learning new words. To foster vocabulary learning you must also help students see the connection between words. Many young children are puzzled by some words that have more than one meaning. They wonder how we can say both that a dog barks and that there is bark on a tree. In fact, *Dorling Kindersley Merriam-Webster's Children's Dictionary* (2000) lists six meanings for *bark*. Some of the most common words, such as *bad*, *ring*, and *catch*, have multiple shades of meaning.

Children can be led to make word connections through a variety of teaching techniques such as word-cluster charts and word collections. These techniques will be examined in classroom contexts in Part II of this book.

Maintaining Vocabulary Knowledge. Children need frequent encounters with words if they are to become a permanent part of the students' vocabularies. That means you have to keep words around for a while. For example, you might designate a specific portion of your word wall to the ten or so new words you teach each week. Students can be encouraged to try using the new words in their writing and speech. When these words are used, orally or in writing, or noted in books, you and the students might make a check mark next to the word on the word wall. In this way, a class's "favorite words" are identified.

"Retired" words can be brought into use periodically throughout the year in simple verbal games. For example, you might write a sentence on the board leaving out a word and give the students several choices of retired words to fill in the blank. This could also be an activity at a center for students to complete independently. You can also use a simple verbal interaction to revisit retired words as students wait in line for lunch or gather on the rug. Ask questions such as "If I say you have the most beautiful hair in the class, would you be horrified or happy?" Or you can dismiss children by using retired vocabulary words as second-grade teacher Shelly Tennett does: "All those wearing a *vibrant* color may return to their seats."

♦ ♦ ♦ Final Thoughts ♦ ♦ ♦

Vocabulary development plays a significant role in reading comprehension throughout school. The foundation for a rich and varied vocabulary begins in the preschool years and continues throughout life. However, vocabulary development cannot be left to chance. Research suggests that an effective vocabulary program includes

- ♦ many opportunities for young students to hear high-quality literature read aloud,
- ♦ a classroom context that fosters word consciousness,
- ♦ explicit teaching of individual words,
- ♦ instruction in word-learning strategies.

Since we know that a broad, deep understanding of and a keen interest in words leads to an enhanced ability to read and write effectively, the result will make the effort worthwhile.

CHAPTER 4

Fluency

The Research on Fostering Reading Fluency

Reading fluency refers to the ability of readers to read quickly, effortlessly, and efficiently with good, meaningful expression. It means much more than mere accuracy in reading.

—Timothy V. Rasinski

As we step into Carl Porter's second-grade classroom, a small group of students, reading from scripts, performs a spirited rendition of *The True Story of the 3 Little Pigs* by Jon Scieszka (Viking, 1989). The hilarious tale, told from the wolf's perspective, keeps the class listening with rapt attention and glee. Later, Carl debriefs the students about their performance.

Carl: How did you think it went?

Michael: It was okay, but maybe we could have put more expression into it.

Jessica: I think we could have practiced a little more. I still had trouble with a few words.

Jerome: Yeah, I could've read a little faster, but my part was funny so everyone laughed.

Carl: Yes, you really did a good job with your expression and that made the audience really laugh. How do the rest of you feel you did with your expression?

Darnel: [*Makes a face.*] Maybe I could have read in a more interesting way.

Jessica: Yeah, we didn't have enough time to practice and I needed to make my part sound more interesting too.

Carl: Okay. I pretty much agree with you about needing to practice more, but the audience sure enjoyed it. Let's think about how expression makes reading more meaningful and interesting as we look at the next story.

These performers are practicing reading fluently through Readers Theater.

Overview of the Chapter

In the preceding snippet of instructional conversation the children touched on three components of oral reading fluency as they evaluated their performance: accuracy, speed, and expression. These components are the focus of this chapter. We define oral reading fluency, explore the research on fluency, and suggest some methods for assessing and teaching for oral reading fluency in the primary grades. We specifically target *oral* reading fluency because we believe it is the foundation of silent reading fluency (Rasinski, 2003, p. 8).

Fluency Defined

Oral reading fluency is regarded as a primary factor in effective reading (NICHHD, 2000a). Children who read slowly, word-by-word, with little expression, have difficulty comprehending and remembering what they read. It is this connection to comprehension that makes fluency most critical. For years, oral reading fluency was neglected in the primary school (Reutzel & Hollingsworth, 1993) because many believed that it was important to move children to silent reading, the most common form of reading for adults, as quickly as possible (Rasinski, 2003, p. 7). However, researchers now suggest that oral reading fluency should play a more prominent role in reading instruction because it leads to better silent reading comprehension (NICHHD; Rasinski; Snow et al., 1998).

According to Johns and Berglund, "Reading fluency is the ability to read with accuracy, expression, comprehension, and appropriate rate" (2002, p. 3). (See Figure 4.1.) These four factors are closely related, and difficulty in any one affects the overall meaning-making system in reading.

> **Figure 4.1**
>
> ### Four Components of Oral Reading Fluency in a Nutshell
>
> 1. **Accuracy:** correct pronunciation of words
> 2. **Expression:** reading in larger phrase chunks and conveying mood or feeling through changing voice tone—pauses, emphases, and pitch variations
> 3. **Comprehension:** prior knowledge of the world and past experience used to interpret, infer, connect with, understand, and evaluate an author's intended meaning
> 4. **Appropriate rate:** speed at which words are correctly pronounced relative to the purposes of the reader
>
> Adapted from Rasinski, 2003.

What Research Says About . . .

The Components of Oral Reading Fluency

In the last two decades, the understanding of what is involved in oral reading fluency has changed significantly (Samuels, 2002). Historically, oral reading fluency was defined only as rapid, automatic, accurate word recognition (LaBerge & Samuels, 1974). Today, researchers typically conceptualize fluency to include comprehending processes as well as expression (NICHHD, 2000a; Samuels; Thurlow & van den Broek, 1997).

First, we discuss accuracy and reading rate, the two components of the traditional view of oral reading fluency. Then, we address expression, a new aspect to consider in fluent oral reading. Comprehension was addressed separately and more thoroughly in Chapter 2; however, it is a thread that is woven throughout the research in this chapter, for, as you will see, comprehension and fluency are inextricably related.

Accuracy and Reading Rate

Accurate and rapid word recognition is the foundation for reading fluency (LaBerge & Samuels, 1974) and is closely tied to comprehension. When a child reads with accuracy, she pronounces words correctly, given the reading context. For example, the word *read* must be pronounced as *reed*, not *red*, when in the context of "He will read the newspaper." The child would only know how to correctly pronounce *read* if she were comprehending the context. Word pronunciation and comprehension interact synergistically. That is, to experience good comprehension, the reader must be able to identify words accurately and easily; to identify and pronounce words correctly, the reader must be able to comprehend the context.

Reading rate refers to the speed of reading, usually determined by the number of words pronounced correctly per minute. This is also an important factor in reading comprehension. Students who read slowly, word-by-word, sounding out many words are giving too much attention at the word level to focus on meaning. By the time they have figured out a difficult word, often they have forgotten what the sentence or paragraph was about. Fleisher, Jenkins, and Pany (1979) explain the relationship between word recognition and comprehension in this way:

> **The basic notion is that individuals possess limited amounts of processing space, and that decoding and comprehension are separate but interrelated tasks both requiring this space. The more processing space consumed by decoding, the less processing space is available for comprehension. Thus, inefficient decoding can detract from comprehension. (p. 45)**

Researchers (e.g., Beck et al., 2002; Zeno, Ivens, Millard, & Duvvuri, 1995) have identified the words that students must be able to read rapidly and accurately. These are the words that occur most often in the English language (e.g., *the, is, into*) or that you would encounter most frequently in everyday life (e.g., *clock, baby, happy, walk*). You may have called these "sight words" or "sight vocabulary." A mere 107 words make up almost half the words in written text (Zeno et al.). Figure 4.2 lists the 107 most frequently used words in written English.

Note how many of the 107 words in Figure 4.2 appear often in the earliest books for younger readers. Note also how often you and your students use these words in your own everyday writing. These would be good words *Pre K – 2nd* on which to focus instruction in preschool through second grade.

While accuracy and speed are necessary for fluent reading, research now

Figure 4.2

The 107 Most Frequently Used Words in Written English

the	as	but	about	your	how	also	back
of	are	by	up	which	than	down	where
and	they	were	said	do	two	make	know
to	with	one	out	then	may	now	little
a	be	all	if	many	only	way	such
in	his	she	some	these	most	each	even
is	at	when	would	no	its	called	much
that	or	an	so	time	made	did	our
it	from	their	people	been	over	just	must
was	had	there	them	who	see	after	
for	I	her	other	like	first	water	
you	not	can	more	could	new	through	
he	have	we	will	has	very	get	
on	this	what	into	him	my	because	

Zeno, Ivens, Millard, & Duvvuri, 1995.

suggests that they are not sufficient indications of fluent reading of continuous text. Schreiber (1987) suggested that expression is also a critical component in oral reading fluency.

Expression

Oral language is more than uttering words. It also includes body language, such as hand gestures or facial expressions. Try explaining a spiral without using your hands! Try scolding your students with a smile on your face!

In addition, there are two aspects to how oral language sounds that carry meaning. One is phrasing, and the other is tone of voice. Both of these are features of expression in fluent oral reading.

Phrasing

We do not speak with equal spacing between words; this would sound robotic. *Tomorrow/ we/ are/ going/ to/ breakfast/ with/ a/ friend.* Instead, we tend to speak in phrases, slightly pausing between chunks of words that naturally go together: *Tomorrow/ we are going to breakfast/ with a friend.* The words usually go together, or chunk, in noun phrases, verb phrases, or prepositional phrases.

chunk

Effective readers also read in phrase chunks. For example, you might read the following sentence in longer chunks: *Instead/ we tend to read in phrases/ chunking words that go together.* The longer the chunk of words read together, the more effective the reading. You could also have read the above sentence in smaller phrase chunks: *Instead/ we tend/ to read in phrases/ chunking words/ that go together.* Notice how this sounds choppy compared with the same sentence that was divided into longer phrase chunks. Good readers have a variety of phrases that they recognize and can read almost as quickly as individual words. They can read groups of phrases together, making comprehension easier, because it leaves more room for the reader's attention to focus on meaning, rather than on looking at words. If the reading is in small chunks, as in word-by-word reading or in short phrases, then the reading sounds choppy and unnatural, and comprehension is compromised.

The boundaries between phrases are usually marked with a pause. The pauses between phrases are very subtle and are usually accompanied by changes in voice tone.

Voice

The second feature of expression is the voice tone with which words are spoken. Emphasis, pitch, and volume are qualities of voice tone. The relatively neutral words "I'm glad you came today" can be voiced in either sarcastic or joyful tones to communicate the intended message. A sarcastic tone would make the words mean the opposite—"Humph, are we ever sorry you showed up today!"

Further, the speaker can emphasize different words in the same statement to communicate different meanings. As you read the sentences below, emphasizing the words in bold print, notice how the emphasis causes your voice to be pitched higher on some words and lower on others. Notice also how this changes the meaning of the sentence.

- I'm glad **you** came today.   (as opposed to someone else coming)

- **I'm** glad you came today.   (Others may not be as glad.)

- I'm **glad** you came today.   (as opposed to being sorry)

- I'm glad you came **today**.   (Another day would not have been as preferable.)

You can also notice how the pitch of your voice often goes up when you read a question: Will you be going with us today? Conversely, the pitch of your voice goes down at the end of this sentence: Yes, I will be going with you today.

The volume with which something is spoken can also tell you "volumes." A sentence pitched either at a scream or at a whisper might mean something different, depending on what words are emphasized.

Pauses, emphases, and pitch variations are voiced features of oral language that give it meaning. In fact, you've probably heard that "it's not *what* you say, it's *how* you say it" that counts.

Unfortunately, written language is not able to convey completely the features of phrasing or voice tone. Punctuation helps, but it is not sufficient to communicate all the nuances of spoken language. Therefore, young readers have to learn how to infer appropriate phrasing and voice to read orally with expression. And that means they must be tuning in to the nuances of meaning in the text. Here's that fluency/comprehension connection again. In fact, researchers have found that a useful indicator of fluent comprehension is the ability to read a passage with expression (Dowhower, 1987; Herman, 1985; Su, Samuels, & Flom, 1999). Inferring expression connects a dynamic, three-dimensional world of oral language with the flat, two-dimensional world of written language so that the reader can interpret and "hear" the full meaning of the printed word.

What the Research Says About . . .
Assessing and Teaching for Oral Reading Fluency

In this section we give a sample of some ways classroom teachers can assess and teach for fluency development in young readers. If you are providing a comprehensive early literacy program with opportunities for read-alouds, shared reading, guided reading, and writing workshop, you are probably already using a major tool for assessing fluency: running records. And, you are probably already providing opportunities for students to develop reading fluency throughout your reading block.

Assessing Oral Reading Fluency

S. Jay Samuels, one of the leading researchers in the area of fluency, wrote, "The critical test of fluency is the ability to decode a text and comprehend it at the same time" (2002, p. 180). There are many high-quality informal reading inventories available to do this, such as the *Qualitative Reading Inventory-3* (Leslie & Caldwell, 2001) or the *Developmental Reading Inventory* (Beaver, 1997). However, we believe that you can quickly and effectively assess fluency using an informal assessment tool already at hand in your classroom: running records. With running records you can assess word reading accuracy, reading rate, and expression.

If you are unfamiliar with this tool, we strongly suggest you refer to Marie Clay's book *Running Records for Classroom Teachers* (2000). Running records are an individualized assessment, and you take them sitting beside a student while he or she reads a text. While there are special forms for taking running records, all you really need is a plain sheet of paper and knowledge of a few conventions for recording what the student is doing as he or she reads. Figure 4.3 is a brief review of the conventions for taking a running record of oral reading.

Figure 4.3

Conventions for Taking a Running Record of Oral Reading

- Make a check for each word the student reads correctly. If a student read five words in a row correctly, it would look like this:

    ✓　　✓　　✓　　✓　　✓

- The number and layout of check marks on your paper should correspond to the number and layout of words read correctly on each page of the student's text. For example, if there are two lines of text on a page, with five words in one line and four in the next, you would make two lines of checks on your paper, with five checks for the first line and four for the second line. It is helpful to put the page number beside the first line you record for each page:

    p. 3　✓　　✓　　✓　　✓　　✓
    　　　✓　　✓　　✓　　✓

- If the child makes an error, try to capture as well as you can what the child said, draw a line under it, and write the word from the text below the line. If the student reads too fast for you to do this during the running record, you can go back and fill it in afterward.

    p. 5　✓　<u>dade</u>　✓　　✓　　✓
    　　　　 Daddy

- Words are not counted as incorrect if they are repeated or self-corrected. Words the student repeats are noted with *R* and a number to indicate the number of times it was repeated. Words that are self-corrected are noted with *sc*:

    p. 6　✓　　✓　<u>Daddy\sc</u>　<u>to\R2</u>　✓

- Sometimes a student rereads a section of words, and you show it in this way:

    p. 6　✓　　✓　<u>Daddy\sc</u>　<u>to\R2</u>　✓

Accuracy

Here's how to assess accuracy by taking running records of oral reading.

1. **Take a running record.** Have a student read an instructional text. For a kindergartner or first grader, the text should be one you have read with the student recently in guided reading. For more-experienced readers in first and second grade, a new text at the anticipated instructional level will work.

2. **Calculate the accuracy rate.** See Figure 4.4 for directions. Young readers need to be able to read 90 percent of the words accurately to sustain fluency (Clay, 1993; Gillet & Temple, 2000). Another way to say this is

Words are counted as incorrect if they are

- **omitted.** Words skipped or not read are incorrect; if a student skips a whole line, each word is counted as incorrect. Record a horizontal dash on your paper to indicate that a word was omitted and go back and fill in the word from the text underneath it:

p. 7	✓	—	✓	✓	(1 error)
	Baby	Bear	is	lost	

- **substituted.** If a child reads *mom* for *mother*, it is incorrect, even though it maintains the meaning of the sentence:

p. 2	✓	mom	✓	✓	✓	(1 error)
		mother				

- **unsuccessful attempts** to sound out or pronounce words. If a student reads *sop* for *soup*, it is counted as an error:

p. 3	✓	✓	s-s-s\sop	✓	✓	(1 error)
			soup			

- **not attempted.** If the student comes to a word and stops longer than three seconds, the student is told the word, and it is counted as an error. You record a *T* (for "told") on the bottom next to the actual word in the text:

p. 3	✓	✓	—	✓	✓	(1 error)
			soup\T			

- It is helpful to remember that anything the child does is recorded *above* the line. The actual text or the teacher responses are recorded *below* the line.

Figure 4.4

Calculating Accuracy Rate

To determine a student's error ratio after taking a running record, divide the total number of words the student read by the number of errors, not counting repetitions and self-corrections.

For example, if a student reads 79 words and makes four errors (79 ÷ 4 = 19.75), the error ratio is 1:19.75 words. This corresponds to an accuracy rate of 95 percent. This book or selection is relatively easy for the student to read with word accuracy, and it means she probably understands the story fairly well.

A student who reads 79 words and makes 11 errors (79 ÷ 11 = 7.18) has an error ratio of 1:7, or an accuracy rate of about 86 percent. This book or selection is too hard for this student. There are too many words that she cannot read accurately, and this probably means her comprehension is compromised.

that young readers should not be making more than one error for every ten words. This is the error ratio.

3. **Analyze the errors.** Determine to what extent the student can recognize the high-frequency words used most often in English or what difficulties the student might have with decoding.

To analyze a student's errors, you can eyeball the running record and get an idea of how well a student recognizes the 107 most common words (see Figure 4.2) and others. For example, when a kindergarten student reads a simple text with one or two lines of print on each page, consistently making errors like these:

I	like	my	home.
My	home	is	here.

you know that this student still needs much practice recognizing common words. He needs to read lots of books at the early levels to build up his "sight vocabulary." The best way to build up automatic word recognition is to spend a lot of time reading (Samuels, 2002). The research evidence is very clear: One of the major differences between poor and good readers is the difference in the total quantity of time they have spent reading (e.g., Allington, 1977; Biemiller, 1977; Stanovich, 1986).

Conversely, if you find a student making frequent errors that contain many of the same letters or letter patterns as the word in the text, like these:

rides	skates	bucket	lovely	further
ride	skating	basket	clever	farther

then you know that the student may need more explicit instruction in decoding as well as more time to practice reading. Building a corpus of words that can be recognized quickly and automatically and learning how to decode unfamiliar words are key ingredients for accurate, efficient reading.

As you are taking your running record of oral reading, you can also assess reading rate and expression. There is really nothing more practical than an assessment tool that assesses several areas at once.

Reading Rate

Before telling you how to assess reading rate, we must begin with a caution. While we strongly support fostering strong word-recognition skills, we hesitate to put too much emphasis on speed at the early levels. Young children who are just learning to read typically need to slow down in order to learn how to coordinate eye movements left to right and to match speech with print in a one-to-one manner, using a finger to guide them. These are important prerequisites in early literacy development, and mastery of directionality and one-to-one matching indicates a child knows how English print works. Young children at the emergent level should use their fingers to point to words.

In addition, since young readers are just beginning to build a corpus of sight words, they need many opportunities to see those words in the context of continuous text before they can rapidly and automatically recognize them on sight (e.g., Samuels, 2002). Therefore, don't expect emerging and early readers to read new text quickly, even at their instructional level, unless it is a very familiar text. It is not productive to try to assess reading rate for typical kindergarten or first-grade students who are still building a vocabulary of sight words.

With that said, we also need to provide a caution in the opposite direction. The slow, finger-pointing reading can become habituated and can actually prevent fluency from developing. Therefore, once young children have securely grasped directionality and one-to-one matching, you can begin encouraging "reading with the eyes" of familiar, easy text. This will naturally speed up the reading. Smooth, well-coordinated eye movements across the

> ### Figure 4.5
>
> ## Calculating Reading Rate
>
> The easiest way to calculate words read per minute is to use a stopwatch. After you have finished taking a running record for accuracy, ask the student to reread a section of the text again.
>
> 1. Begin timing the student's reading as soon as he starts reading.
> 2. Tell the student to stop reading when the stopwatch indicates one minute has passed.
> 3. Make a slash mark on the running record to indicate where the student began reading and ended.
> 4. Count up the number of words the student read in that one minute.

page are the foundation for efficient reading rate. Typically progressing second graders might need to use their fingers only if they slow down to carefully analyze an unknown word. In general, second graders are ready to be assessed on reading rate.

The steps to follow to calculate reading rate are listed in Figure 4.5. We suggest you calculate rates only once or twice across the year in second grade, either to ensure that students are reading fast enough to carry meaning across longer texts or to report reading rate to your district and parents if it is required. For students who are not making expected progress, you may want to monitor reading rate more frequently.

You will probably take a running record every two to four weeks to monitor students' progress in guided reading texts. That should be fine for gauging error rates to guide your instruction around word learning and decoding. It will also be sufficient to give you up-to-date information about how well students are reading with expression, a good indicator of comprehension (Dowhower, 1987; Herman, 1985; Su et al., 1999).

Second-grade norms for reading rate (Hasbrouck & Tindal, 1992) are listed in Figure 4.6. It shows the number of words a second grader should be able to read correctly per minute at three points across the school year: fall, winter, and spring. It also also shows what percentile a student falls into with particular reading rates: 75th, 50th, and 25th percentiles. For example, if a second grader read 120 words per minute in January, he would fall into the top quartile. That means he is reading faster than typical students in second grade. A second grader who read 80 words per minutes in January would be at the 50th percentile, or average for second grade. The norms for second grade are only valid and reliable if the second grader is able to read text at the second-grade level. These norms should not be used for second graders who are reading below grade level.

Figure 4.6

Norms in Oral Reading Fluency for Grade 2 (Medians)

Words Correct per Minute

Percentile	Fall	Winter	Spring
75	82	106	124
50	53	78	94
25	23	46	65

Note: From Hasbrouck and Tindal (1992, p. 4). Copyright 1992 by the Council for Exceptional Children. Reprinted by permission.

Expression

Expression is usually assessed using a rubric. Figure 4.7 is the rubric used in the National Assessment of Educational Progress (NAEP) oral reading study given as part of the 1992 NAEP (Pinnell, 1995). It asks the assessor to rate phrasing as well as "expressive interpretation" in oral reading. You can think

Figure 4.7

The NAEP Oral Reading Fluency Scale

Level 4 Reads primarily in larger, meaningful phrase groups. Although some regressions, repetitions, and deviations from text may be present, these do not appear to detract from the overall structure of the story. Preservation of the author's syntax is consistent. Some or most of the story is read with expressive interpretation.

Level 3 Reads primarily in three- or four-word phrase groups. Some smaller groupings may be present. However, the majority of phrasing seems appropriate and preserves the syntax of the author. Little or no expressive interpretation is present.

Level 2 Reads primarily in two-word phrases with some three- or four-word groupings. Some word-by-word reading may be present. Word groupings may seem awkward and unrelated to larger content of sentence or passage.

Level 1 Reads primarily word by word. Occasional two-word or three-word phrases may occur, but these are infrequent and/or they do not preserve meaningful syntax.

Note: From U.S. Department of Education, National Center for Education Statistics by G. S. Pinnell, J. J. Pikulski, K. K. Wixson, J. R. Campbell, P. B. Gough, & A. S. Beatty, 1995, p. 15.

of "expressive interpretation" as the features of voice tone: emphases, pauses, and variations in pitch and volume.

Note that an emerging reader reading a level 1 text, with enthusiasm and expression, can rate a 4 on the oral reading scale as easily as a second grader reading a level 28. The difference may be that the emerging reader has read the level 1 text many times to achieve the phrasing and expression. A second grader, on the other hand, should be able to pick up an unknown text on his or her instructional level and read with phrasing and expression. No reader can be expected to read with phrasing and expression when the text level is too hard, or the content of the selection is outside his or her experiences and concepts.

Directions for using the NAEP rubric are listed in Figure 4.8 on the next page. Keep in mind that one of the difficulties of using a rubric is that different raters may have different interpretations of rating categories. We strongly recommend that you meet with other teachers who are trying to assess oral reading fluency with this rubric and establish inter-rater agreement before assessing phrasing and appropriate expression on your own.

Figure 4.8

How to Use the NAEP Oral Reading Fluency Scale

1. While taking a running record of a student's oral reading of easy or instructional text, make a mental note of how the reading sounds, listening for appropriate voice tone: emphases, pauses, and variations in pitch and volume.

2. Make slashes on the running record to indicate words that are read in phrased groupings. Make another mental note of how well the reading preserves smooth, flowing language syntax, as opposed to sounding choppy or awkward.

3. After taking the running record, count up the number of phrased groups on the running record. Did the student read primarily in phrases or word by word? If your running record indicates very few phased groupings, score the student a level 1 on the rubric.

4. If the running record indicates quite a few phrased groupings, tally the phrased groupings that fell into these categories: phrased groups of more than four words, phrased groups of three or four words, and phrased groups of two words.

5. Check the rubric to find the category that best describes the overall number of words the student used most frequently in phrased groupings.

6. Then check to see if the category you selected to describe the number of words in phrased groupings corresponds to your mental note about how smooth the reading sounded.

7. And finally, check the category again to see if it fits with the description of "expressive interpretation" you noted in the student's voice tone.

Note: From U.S. Department of Education, National Center for Education Statistics by G. S. Pinnell, J. J. Pikulski, K. K. Wixson, J. R. Campbell, P. B. Gough, & A. S. Beatty, 1995, p. 15.

Teaching for Oral Reading Fluency

Now that you know how to assess for reading accuracy, rate, and expression, you are ready to match fluency instruction to your students' varying needs. Once again, we emphasize that to teach fluency (and comprehension and vocabulary), you do not have to add another layer to what you are already doing. Instead, you integrate teaching and learning opportunities throughout your regularly scheduled early literacy activities. The research on learning in general, and reading specifically, supports the range of practices found in a comprehensive early literacy program.

Conditions for Effective Learning

The conditions for effective learning in general also apply to teaching for fluency in the early literacy program. (See Bransford, Brown, & Cocking, 1999, for a thorough review of principles for teaching and learning; Samuels, 2002, p. 172). First, students must be *motivated* to attend to the task they need to learn. Second, students need *explicit instruction* in how to do the task, and third, students need *extended practice* using the learning. These conditions for human learning apply to almost any task: playing basketball, learning a musical instrument, making a bed, tying your shoes, and so on. In terms of fluency development, the implications for instruction are

1. **Motivation:** Students need lots of reading material that they find interesting and pleasurable to read.
2. **Instruction:** Students need explicit, specific instruction in how to read fluently with phrasing and appropriate expression. They also need instruction in decoding, word-analysis skills, and word building.
3. **Extended practice:** Students need opportunities for extended practice of fluent reading in ways that are motivating and authentic. They need texts that are on easy and instructional levels to accomplish this.

These three conditions for effective learning can be met in a comprehensive early literacy program that includes opportunities for you to teach explicitly, combined with opportunities for students to practice reading in ways that are fun, interesting, and motivational.

Comprehensive Early Literacy Program Defined

Effective literacy programs have been proposed recently in several popular books for teachers. Michael Pressley, in his book *Reading Instruction That Works: The Case for Balanced Teaching* (2002), argues for reading instruction that entails "both skills instruction and holistic reading and writing experiences" (p. 2). In their book *Guided Reading* (1996), Irene Fountas and Gay Su Pinnell outline four contexts for reading that provide four levels of teacher support and allow for both explicit teaching and reading practice: read-alouds, shared reading, guided reading, and independent reading. Linda Dorn, Cathy French, and Tammy Jones also advocate for these four reading contexts in their book *Apprenticeship in Literacy* (1998). Jan Kristo and Rosemary Bamford describe a "comprehensive framework" in their book *Nonfiction in Focus* (2004) that includes these four contexts for reading as well as a new context, reading discovery circles.

Here's how the conditions for effective human learning are met through a comprehensive early literacy program:

♦ Through *reading aloud* to students you show them how fluent reading sounds, and you cultivate their interest and enjoyment in reading.

♦ In *shared* and *guided reading* you have opportunities to provide explicit, specific instruction in how to read in phrases with appropriate expression.

♦ During *independent reading* and *performance reading* (e.g., Readers Theater) students have opportunities for extended practice of reading.

♦ Of course, when you choose a wide range of fun and interesting *fiction and nonfiction texts* that are on young children's interest and reading levels, you further motivate their interest in reading, learning to read, and in practicing reading in fun and interesting ways.

♦ Finally, in a comprehensive early literacy program there are many opportunities for students to talk about the books they read. Whatever you call them—literature circles, book clubs, discovery circles—they serve an important role in developing comprehension, vocabulary, and fluency by helping students develop deeper understandings of both the texts they read/hear and the text structures.

There is now a common understanding about the contexts necessary for a balanced, comprehensive early literacy program that supports the conditions for learning: motivation, explicit instruction, and extended practice. Note that all the authors mentioned here also include writing in their frameworks for literacy. We strongly agree that writing and reading are inseparable in early literacy teaching and learning. However, as we are focusing specifically on the components of comprehension, vocabulary, and fluency, we refer only to the elements of a comprehensive early literacy program related to reading.

It would be hard not to meet the conditions for human learning in your classroom if you provide the balanced, comprehensive early literacy program described above. All the instructional elements that support and promote learning are present. There are two other important research findings that have implications for teaching fluency and that support the use of a comprehensive early literacy program: time spent reading and repeated readings.

Time Spent Reading

The research literature strongly suggests that the total amount of reading done in the beginning stages of learning to read has a powerful effect on reading achievement (see Samuels, 2002, for a thorough review of this research). Researchers theorize that one of the benefits of lots of reading is that students encounter the same common words in story after story, building a corpus of words that they can immediately recognize. The implication of this finding is that there needs to be substantial time during the school day for students to engage in the reading of continuous text at their level. You automatically provide more time for students to read when you include shared, guided, and independent reading in the schedule.

However, the research is also clear that just flipping through books, looking at pictures, does not produce more effective reading (NICHHD, 2000a; Samuels, 2002). Traditional "silent sustained reading" in classrooms for young children has not proven very effective because the children cannot yet read many texts. Therefore, you may need to structure the independent reading time a little more. The best way to ensure that students have books they can read is to keep collections of books at the easy and instructional levels for each of your guided reading groups. Many teachers keep "book boxes," small plastic tubs filled with easy and instructional texts. The advantage of having students reread easy books on their level is that they are actually engaging in another effective practice supported by research: repeated reading.

Repeated Reading

Repeated reading is a specific instructional technique that appears to have a significant and positive effect on fluency at a variety of grade levels (NICHHD, 2000a; Rasinski, 2003; Samuels, 2002). Repeated reading requires students to read and reread a text many times to improve reading fluency. The technique was found to have a significant positive effect on word recognition, reading speed, and comprehension (NICHHD). David LaBerge and S. Jay Samuels at the University of Minnesota and at Harvard University pioneered it in 1974. In the two decades since the method was first introduced, more than 100 studies have consistently found that repeated reading practice produces statistically significant improvement in all components of fluent reading (Samuels, 2002).

When you think about it, reading the same text over and over is a form of extended practice, one of the key conditions for effective learning. But wouldn't children get bored doing this and be less motivated to read? Not if the conditions for repeated reading are right. Timothy V. Rasinski devoted a chapter in his book *The Fluent Reader* to methods for providing repeated reading practice in fun and interesting contexts. Readers Theater and Radio Reading are two methods that encourage students to read and reread a familiar text in order to perform for an audience. We suggest that repeated readings of shared-reading text are another form of engaging young students in repeated reading in a fun and expressive way. Cross-age book buddies, recorded books, and choral reading are other ways to implement the technique of repeated reading appropriately in classrooms for young children. You'll see some of these methods in action in Part II.

◆ ◆ ◆ Final Thoughts ◆ ◆ ◆

Fluent oral reading plays a significant role in effective reading instruction in preschool to second-grade classrooms because it provides the critical foundation for later silent reading. Accuracy, speed, and expression are key components of fluency for both assessment and instruction. However, we hesitate to put too much emphasis on speed at the early levels. Young children who are just learning to read typically need to slow down in order to learn how to coordinate eye movements left to right and to match speech with print in a one-to-one manner, using a finger to guide them.

In addition, since young readers are just beginning to build a corpus of sight words, they need many opportunities to see those words in the context of continuous text before they can rapidly and automatically recognize them on sight (see for example, Samuels, 2002). It is not productive to try to assess reading rate for typical kindergarten or first-grade students who are still building a vocabulary of sight words.

Furthermore, you cannot really say that a young reader is fluent if he or she does not also comprehend the message in the text. For this reason, comprehension is now also considered a critical component in fluency.

It is hard to say which comes first in the development of effective reading: rapid, automatic word recognition or comprehension. Rapid, automatic word recognition facilitates comprehending processes by making it possible for the reader to concentrate on meaning, not decoding. At the same time, comprehension fuels word recognition processes by helping the reader predict word choice (i.e., vocabulary) and pronunciation (i.e., accuracy). It is likely that rapid word recognition, knowledge of word meanings, and comprehension are separate but interdependent subprocesses that operate synergistically as one meaning-making system in both reading and writing. That is why it is often difficult to separate them during assessment and teaching.

PART II

Research
Into
Practice

CHAPTER 5

Changes in Children's Literacy Development

Implications for Instruction

Erika and Tom are the parents of seven-year-old Simon, a second grader, and a four-year-old preschooler, Peter. As parents, Erika and Tom have watched their children's literacy development with wonder. They marvel that while Peter spends lots of time singing nursery rhymes that he has learned at school, he occasionally demonstrates amazing abilities. While decorating Valentine's Day cookies with Erika, Peter picked up a candy heart and said, "Look Mom. This one says, 'my girl.'" As Peter dissolved into a fit of giggles, Erika wondered how Peter had learned to read the words *my* and *girl*. She remembered Simon's journey toward literacy and how he had also amazed his parents on occasion. As Erika and Peter finished the cookies, Erika decided to keep a journal of Peter's and Simon's literacy progress. She felt that one day the boys would find their literacy growth as fascinating as she did.

One of the pleasures of teaching young children is the opportunity to observe and guide literacy development. Teachers witness experiences such as Erika's regularly. They know that these demonstrations of knowledge come at odd times as well as during structured lessons. Teachers must be aware of growth that occurs in their lessons but must also be aware of each child's ability to take what has been learned and apply it. In order to meet the needs of the children in their classrooms, teachers must be constantly alert to changes and growth in children's literacy development. Carefully recording progress, as Erika decided to do, allows classroom teachers to plan effectively for continued growth.

Overview of the Chapter

Young readers' developmental needs change as they move through the early years, from preschool to second grade, and instruction must match not only their cognitive development but also their social, emotional, and physical changes. In this chapter, we present broad and general descriptions of how young readers develop over the early years. Understanding how young children typically develop literacy knowledge will help you adapt instruction in comprehension, vocabulary, and fluency to young children's changing needs.

Developmental Changes in Reading

Young readers go through marked changes in reading development. The changes can be characterized in stages, commonly referred to as *prereading*, *emergent*, *early*, and *transitional* (e.g., Dorn & Soffos, 2001; Dorn et al., 1998; Fountas & Pinnell, 1996, 1999; Lyon & Moore, 2003; Mooney, 1990; New Zealand Department of Education, 1994; Parkes, 2000).

A note of caution: Attempts to neatly tuck young readers into reading developmental phases are sometimes problematic at best; most students tend to demonstrate characteristics of several categories at once. They are changing quickly over time in ways that make it hard to keep up with their developing needs. Therefore, categories for reading development provide only rough guidelines for curriculum planning or instruction. You still need to look closely at individual, unique student needs when planning instruction. With that in mind, here are the broad categories of reading development.

Prereading

This stage is marked by a child's ability to listen to a book read aloud and even to "retell" a favorite book by turning pages and "reading" the pictures.

Emergent Reading

Children at this stage are able to point to words in text, matching voice to print and moving left-to-right across the page. Emergent readers know some words, especially their own names and the names of favorite people and pets. They know how letters are different from words and how letters differ from one another. Typically, emergent reading begins toward the middle and end of kindergarten. However, it is also typical to find preschoolers or first graders who are "emerging." Emergent readers can read books at level A (1) that have a highly predictable text structure (e.g., *I can run. I can hop. I can jump.*) and pictures that provide strong clues to the meaning.

> The guided reading levels included here are from *Guided Reading: Good First Teaching for All Children* by Irene Fountas and Gay Su Pinnell (1996).

Early Reading

This stage is marked by the ability to read longer texts with less repetitive sentence structures. Early readers recognize and read some words by sight, and they know many letter sounds. In addition, early readers have strategies to monitor and self-correct reading errors; they are able to notice letter clusters (e.g., /th/, /or/) and word parts (e.g., *ate*, *ing*, *ig*) that they can use to help them figure out unknown words. Typically, beginning and midyear first graders fall within the early reader category. They read texts at levels B (2) through D (5/6) at the beginning of the year and levels E (7/8) through G (11/12) by midyear.

Transitional Reading

Transitional readers are able to read more-complex text and to decode longer, more-complex words automatically. Transitional readers read faster with more-automatic problem solving, and reading out loud changes to silent reading. With increased reading rate and efficiency in problem solving, transitional readers can sustain attention to meaning over longer stretches of text, such as chapter books. Typically, students at the end of first grade and throughout second grade are transitional readers. They read text levels H or I (13/14 or 15/16) at the end of first grade, levels J or K (18/20 or 22) at the beginning of second grade, and levels L to M (24 to 28) by the end of second grade.

Changes in Instruction Across the Early Grades

In general, teaching moves from providing massive amounts of exposure to books through read-alouds and shared reading in the preschool and kindergarten years to more explicit teaching of comprehending processes, vocabulary, and fluency by first and second grades. Changes in teaching follow changes not only in children's reading development, but also in their social and emotional development. Here are brief descriptions of the instructional changes you will see in action in the chapters in Part II. Note that these are descriptions of instruction for typically progressing children at these grade levels. Every classroom is likely to have learners at various stages in both reading and social-emotional development, and primary teachers need to be skilled in moving through the range of instructional practices needed to teach children at differing levels of ability and development.

Preschoolers

Preschoolers benefit from exposure to books read aloud to them and from conversations that help them make meaning from text. They also learn from play with language through songs and rhymes, from exploring letter forms through manipulatives, and from learning to recognize and write their own names and friends' names.

Kindergartners

Kindergartners continue to benefit from exposure to conversation about books read aloud and about the vocabulary in those books. However, they also benefit from repeated reading of text in a shared reading context that includes further talk about meaning and vocabulary. During shared reading, the children and teacher read an enlarged text (big books or overhead projections) together. The teacher reads the text at first. Then, as the text is reread on subsequent days, the children become more familiar with the text, and they are able to follow along and read with the teacher. Because the story is familiar now, the children can more easily learn how to look closely at letters and words in print, recognize and read letters and known words in familiar shared-reading text, and link vocabulary concepts.

Big books

Kindergartners also benefit from interactive writing lessons. During interactive writing, the teacher and children share the task of writing. The children write letters, words, and sounds that they know, and the teacher writes the rest. The teacher demonstrates and teaches new sounds, words, and letters. Usually by midyear, some kindergartners are ready to transition into reading simple, repetitive texts (e.g., *Here is a cat. Here is a dog.*) on their own. The pictures on each page are clues to the one new word on each page, and the books are constructed so that many of the words are the "high-frequency" ones (e.g., *and, is, the*) learned during shared reading and interactive writing.

Some K students

Through reading these simple texts on their own, kindergartners learn other important concepts about print, such as the need to match each word said aloud with the exact word on the page, how to move left to right across the line of print, and how to return to the left-hand side of the next line of print (return sweep). Once kindergartners have a corpus of known high-frequency words and they can control one-to-one match, left-to-right directionality, and return sweep, they are ready for the next leap in instruction: guided reading.

First Graders

First graders still need conversations about meaning and vocabulary in the books read aloud to them or in a shared-reading context. However, because they now can read some books themselves, guided reading lessons become the heart of the instructional reading program in first grade. As text levels increase in complexity and length, guided reading lessons focus on explicit teaching of more-complex comprehending processes, vocabulary, and developing fluency in longer and more complex texts.

Second Graders

Second graders are much more independent, especially if they are taught explicitly how to manage themselves, tasks, and time. They typically read longer books but need repeated practice learning to use comprehending processes effectively and to read fluently—orchestrating speed and expression. Second graders need opportunities to practice, practice, practice through independent reading for guided and literature study groups, through reading for content area topics, and through many opportunities to read orally for a specific audience. But they also need explicit instruction during guided and shared reading in how to apply comprehending and fluency processes on more-complex texts, including a variety of nonfiction text structures.

Research-Based Considerations That Span the Grades

Exposure to and conversations about books as well as explicit teaching are hallmarks of high-quality instruction in the early years. Human beings learn through social interaction and through language, in particular. This is what distinguishes us from all other mammals. In Chapter 6 you will see how children learn through talking, and you will explore talk as a vehicle for teaching.

Research has converged significantly on the issue of time spent reading—it is a necessary condition for young readers to develop effective comprehension, vocabulary, and fluency skills (Duke & Pearson, 2002; Graves & Watts-Taffe, 2002; Rasinski, 2003; Samuels, 2002). Because very young learners do not yet read themselves, you will see how teachers meet this research-based condition through read-alouds, shared reading, and interactive writing. In chapters 7, 8, and 9 you will see reading and writing everywhere in the classrooms we profile, integrated naturally throughout the day, upping the ante on "time spent reading."

The research has also determined the elements of effective instruction. Researchers cited in Part I outlined research-based instructional models for explicit teaching of comprehension, vocabulary, and fluency. Nell Duke and P. David Pearson (2002) outlined an instructional model for teaching comprehending processes. Isabel Beck and her colleagues (2002) outlined an instructional sequence for teaching vocabulary words to young readers. Timothy V. Rasinski (2003) described four steps for building reading fluency. Although these models differ in terms of purpose, they embrace a similar instructional sequence, outlined in Figure 5.1.

You will see this sequence of instruction in several of the classrooms described in chapters 7, 8, and 9.

> **Figure 5.1**
>
> **Instructional Sequence for Teaching Comprehending, Vocabulary, and Fluency**
>
> 1. Explicit modeling and explanation of the strategy, word, or skill to be learned.
> 2. Collaborative and/or guided practice with the strategy, word, or skill to be learned.
> 3. Independent practice with the strategy, word, or skill.
> 4. Periodic review of the strategy, word, or skill by the teacher and students.
>
> Adapted from Rasinski, 2003.

◆ ◆ ◆ Final Thoughts ◆ ◆ ◆

You may already be implementing many of the research-based instructional practices that we outline in the subsequent chapters in Part II. We hope these chapters help you build more-explicit rationales for your work.

CHAPTER 6

Teaching and Learning Through Talk

Creating a Rich Context for Literacy Instruction

W here do they put the sun at night?" "Why does the moon follow us?" "Why do giraffes have such long necks?" Young children are filled with wonder and ask endless questions. Adults talk to children to answer their questions and help them learn about the world. Many of our first learning experiences happen through talk. As the teachers at one elementary school discovered, young children aren't the only ones who learn through talk!

The teachers at Central Primary School participated in a yearlong class for teachers in their school district. The teachers explored together how to teach shared and guided reading and how to integrate comprehension, vocabulary, and fluency instruction. The teachers felt that the most important outcomes of the course for them were that they developed a common language for talking about reading, and that they were reminded of the value of talk.

Ralph Peterson (1992) wrote,

> **Teachers who are basically educational technicians rely on materials that present a standardized view of the world. They try to motivate students to learn the material, with grades and promotions being the primary rewards. There is no student ownership. . . .**
>
> **In dialogue, however, what does and does not happen is controlled by the people involved. Meaning arises from collaboration as partners respond to one another in an attempt to uncover meaning and construct an accurate representation of the subject of study. (p. 105)**

construct meaning

The teachers at Central Primary School came to understand the power of talk as Peterson described it. They not only began to use talk as a learning tool in their classrooms, but also started to structure lessons so that talk was central.

Overview of the Chapter

The purpose of this chapter is to explore how talking can facilitate learning in several of the typical instructional contexts in the early primary grades. Conversation becomes a vehicle for teaching during interactive read-aloud, shared reading, writing workshop, and guided reading.

New Essentials for Teaching Reading in PreK–2

Teaching, Learning, and Talk

As the four classrooms we visit in the following sections show, talk is a powerful tool for teaching and learning.

Talking to Learn in Preschool

It is 8 A.M. in Angela Payne's preschool classroom. Rosita, Tiffany, and Tyrone are sitting on the floor watching the class pet, a guinea pig named Jeffery, eat seeds. The children are waiting for Jeffery to finish his breakfast so they can hold him. There is excited conversation about Jeffery as the children watch his every move.

Angela reminds the children of a nonfiction book about guinea pigs she read to them the day before. She asks the children to recall what they learned from the book. She guides the conversation to help them connect the information in the book to their observations and experiences with Jeffery. In their conversations about Jeffery they make connections to Rosita's pet bird and Tyrone's dog.

Tyrone comments that Jeffery eats fast, just like his dog. Rosita notices that both Jeffery and her bird eat seeds. They discuss Jeffery's furry appearance, the way he uses his paws, and his sharp teeth. Tyrone wonders if Jeffery sheds like his dog. Rosita talks about the pretty colors of her bird's feathers. Comments made by one child spark a new bit of insight or curiosity among the listeners. This conversation leads the children to compare and contrast characteristics of their pets, to look at their pets in different ways, and to ask questions of themselves and others.

Quality pre-K K programs

Later that morning, Angela will reread *Guinea Pigs* by Kate Petty (Gloucester Press, 1989) and engage the children in interactive read-aloud. During interactive read-aloud, she will again support the children as they learn to use the words and illustrations in the text to gain meaning. As they read the text, the children will recall their morning conversation. They will confirm information, learn new information, and ask new questions. The children will participate in music and fingerplays that require careful listening and understandings in order to participate fully. During snack time, they will practice the rules of conversation. Lessons often include careful observations and new vocabulary. Talk is helping these children learn how to make sense of their world.

The activities described above are typical of quality preschool and kindergarten programs. Since language development is a goal of preschool and kindergarten, it is expected that a great deal of talk will take place. The

language development a goal

practice of talking freely about a topic or observation should not end with kindergarten. Talk is equally important to children in the primary grades.

Kindergarten, first-grade, and second-grade classrooms are rife with opportunities to learn through talk. Knowing the rules of conversation, being able to reason aloud, and having the ability to communicate orally are skills that children will use throughout their lives. Time spent allowing children to observe, explore, and engage in conversations is time well spent. It allows children to learn from the experience and from one another.

Talk and Shared Reading in Kindergarten

On this first Wednesday of the school year, the children in Donna Cain's kindergarten class are sitting in a cozy circle engaged in a shared-reading lesson. Donna and the children are reading *Wemberly Worried* by Kevin Henkes (Greenwillow, 2000), a story about a mouse who worried about many things, especially the beginning of school. Donna does the reading because most of the children are not yet readers. The children join in during the phrase "worried and worried and worried."

On each page, the children hold conversations about the illustrations. They talk about all of Wemberly's worries and many of their own. The children are encouraged to share their feelings and make many connections to the story. At the end of the story and the conversation, Donna says, "We have read a book together about Wemberly and all of the things she worried about. We have shared our feelings about the beginning of school. In the story, Wemberly felt like many of us! We are going to read lots of books together this year, and I think you will find that you can connect to many of the stories. Sometimes the characters in a story remind us of ourselves or something that happened to us. Sometimes the books remind us of other books we have read, and sometimes they remind us of things and places we know about. Thinking about these connections to what we already know will help us understand new stories."

Donna did not ask the children to wait until the end of the story to share their thoughts and feelings. She knew that by allowing children to talk as the story goes along, she is encouraging active comprehending throughout the story. By listening to their talk, she can direct conversation to details and concepts the children might otherwise miss. The children in Donna's class have been taught the rules of conversation. (See Figure 6.1.) They understand that following these simple rules will allow them to respond and be heard. Through practice sessions with Donna and role-playing, the children have learned to keep to the topic or text being discussed.

Conversation promotes comprehension

Kindergarten is filled with activities such as shared reading, in which the reading process is slowed down in order for the children to grasp the concepts. Reading and writing processes are complex and consist of many skills that must be orchestrated. In order to ensure understanding, it is necessary to pull out and examine skills closely. It is, however, vitally important to then reexamine how each skill promotes an understanding of the whole. Talk surrounding these skill lessons enables students to understand the process and to discuss how the skills they have learned are used while reading and writing.

Talk and Writing Workshop in First Grade

Kim Mendoza plans writing workshop so that there is time for talk during the composing, revising, and editing processes. She is also aware of the importance of talk during conferences and during guided writing lessons. Children in Kim's class are expected to use talk throughout the writing cycle.

Many of the children in Kim's class live in poverty, some are second-language learners, and most have limited access to literacy materials. Kim knows these children are capable learners, but experience has taught her that many of her students will enter first grade with fewer literacy experiences and a more limited vocabulary than their more advantaged peers. The children will need many literacy experiences throughout the school year.

Interactive read-aloud, shared reading, and guided reading are key components in Kim's literacy block. While these contexts are used to systematically and explicitly teach children how to read and write with understanding, Kim will also use science and social studies lessons to teach and reinforce comprehending skills. She will use interactive writing, shared writing, and writing workshop to help the children compose meaningful text.

Visitors to the classroom on this March morning find the children engaged in writing workshop. The children are working on stories about their families—a social studies topic. Knowing the importance of choice of writing topic, Kim has brainstormed possible choices with the children. Together they have decided they could write about their own family, a family event, or retell a story that has been passed down in their family. Most of the children have chosen to tell about a family event. Once the children had settled on a topic, Kim asked them to tell their story to a fellow student. By talking about the story before writing, the children were able to shape their ideas and clarify their thinking. They returned to their seats ready to record their stories.

Four children have gathered with Kim at a table to work on their writing. Maria has drawn an elaborate picture of her grandmother's birthday party. There are many details and bright colors in the drawing. Jamal has drawn a large picture of his new baby sister. Sarah and Matt have each drawn pictures of the park where they both go to play. While there are no words on the papers, Kim will help the children use their drawings to assist with writing.

The children take turns talking about their pictures and rehearsing what they will write. Maria goes first.

Maria: My grandmother's birthday was last Saturday. We ate cake and ice cream. There were lots of candles on her cake!

Jamal: Did she blow them all out and make a wish?

Maria: There were too many for her to blow out, so Jose and I helped her.

Sarah: Who's Jose?

Maria: He is my big brother. He is in third grade so he blew real hard!

Matt: Did your grandmother get lots of presents? I always get lots of presents on my birthday.

Maria: No, she didn't get lots of presents. She just got one.

Matt: Only one!

Maria: Yes, but it was a big present. It was a gift from everyone. We all wrote our names on one big card.

Sarah: What was it? What did she get?

Maria: It was a new computer. She was very surprised because she has never had a computer before. My dad said she could use the computer to send e-mail to our family. Some of them live very far away and my cousin is in college.

Matt: Wow! That's a great present. I hope I get a new computer for my birthday!

Kim and the children have participated in mini-lessons and conferences throughout the year. They have discussed how to make their writing more interesting and meaningful by focusing on one interesting part rather than simply relating events from beginning to end. By allowing conversation,

Kim and the children help Maria see that the gift is an interesting focus for a story.

Kim: Maria has drawn a beautiful picture of her grandmother's birthday party and has told us some interesting things. When you go back to your seat, what will you write about, Maria?

Maria: I will need to tell about her birthday so everyone will know why she got a present.

Kim: Good thinking. In order for your story to make sense, you will need to set the scene so we know why your grandmother is getting such a special present.

Matt: Don't forget to say what she got for a present. That's the best part!

Maria: Okay, and then I want to tell the part about how surprised she was. She even cried. My uncle said not to cry and that he would show her how to use the computer.

Kim: Good. That will help your audience understand how your grandmother was feeling. Do you know how you will end your story, Maria?

Maria: I will say that we all had fun at Grandmother's party.

Jamal: We already know that from your picture. Everybody was smiling.

Maria: Okay, but I want the words to say that too.

Kim: Maria can use words to tell her audience that everyone had fun. Think about what made the party special. What made the party so much fun?

Matt: It's fun to get presents.

Sarah: And eat cake and go to parties and dress up.

Kim: Maria, think about the suggestions your friends made and you can decide if you want to add them to your ending.

The other three children share their drawings and hold conversations to discuss what they will write about. By talking about what they want to say before writing it on paper, the children are able to clarify details and tell their stories in a more coherent way. Kim's support and the mini-lessons she taught are keys to success for all of the children.

As Kim reflected on this lesson, several aspects of it pleased her. Maria and Sarah spoke very limited English at the beginning of the school year. Their spoken English has progressed rapidly. Kim can help these children use their spoken-language abilities to assist with reading and writing. Matt and Jamal entered first grade with limited literacy experiences and vocabularies. These children were given many opportunities to interact with text and to talk with adults and children. They were learning about literacy in authentic contexts and they know that reading and writing need to make sense. In the lesson described above, Kim saw evidence of their growth. Although Maria was able to tell her story coherently, Kim or her assistant will need to conference with Maria as she writes the story. Maria can return to her picture and continue to talk with her teacher and peers to help her decide what she wants to write.

Keep in mind that the lesson described here is simply one lesson in a day filled with literacy learning. During social studies the following day, Kim will ask the children to talk about and read their stories. They will then compare their stories to family life described in their social studies materials. Throughout this social studies unit, Kim and the children have used writing workshop to write about games they play and what they do when they lose a baby tooth—a hot topic with first graders! During read-aloud, she has shared books such as *Throw Your Tooth on the Roof* by Selby Beeler (Houghton Mifflin, 1998) and *Let the Games Begin* by Maya Ajmera and Michael Regan (Charlesbridge, 2000). The class has engaged in the shared reading of the big books and charts that are part of the social studies curriculum. They have had many opportunities for shared and interactive writing, engaged in word study, and learned both sight words and how words work. The success of all of these lessons relies on the quality of the talk.

Talk and Guided Reading in Second Grade

As we walk into Carl Porter's second-grade classroom we see him seated at a kidney-shaped table talking with a small group of students in a guided reading group. Another group of students is in the drama corner rehearsing for their upcoming Readers Theater production. Other students are writing in reader response journals, reading in preparation for a guided reading lesson or for a literature conversation group, or working in pairs to edit drafts.

Carl and his students are exploring the genre of nonfiction. They are also studying amphibians in a science unit, so each day Carl reads the students a book about amphibians as a way to study both comprehending processes for reading nonfiction and the topic of amphibians. Today, he is reading *All About Frogs* by Jim Arnosky (Scholastic, 2002).

Good readers use different comprehending processes on different types of text. Carl wants his students to learn how to use nonfiction text structures as a comprehending strategy. He focused on survey-type nonfiction text in this first lesson about how to read nonfiction. After briefly previewing the book for the students and telling about the author, Carl begins this discussion.

Carl: You know that good readers use different ways to read different types of books. This month I'm going to read nonfiction books aloud. They are organized very differently from stories, and if you know how a book is organized, it helps you read for understanding. *All About Frogs* is called a "survey" nonfiction text because it tells you about a lot of different kinds of frogs and a little bit about frogs in general. The title gives you a clue that this is a survey text. Why does the title give a clue that this is a survey text?

Josh: Well, *all about* means it's going to tell about a lot of things.

Carl: That's a very good inference. If the book were called *Why Frogs Can Jump Far*, it would not be a survey text because it would be only about frogs jumping. In this book, *All About Frogs*, you are going to find out a lot about this amphibian. Let's talk about some things you know about frogs and some things you wonder about frogs.

Kelly: I know that tadpoles change into frogs, but I don't know how they do it.

Mike: Little frogs hop onto our windows at night. I wonder what kind of frogs they are and why they get on the windows. It's kind of creepy.

Ahmed: They get on our patio door, too. Do you think they only get there at night because the light from the house attracts bugs for them to eat? I wonder what frogs do in the winter when there are no bugs out.

Sam: Yeah! Do frogs hibernate?

Carl: These are all great questions. Let's see if we think we can find the answers in this book. I'll read just the first page and you listen to find out all the things the author is going to tell you about frogs.

The first page in the book is a series of questions that operate like advance organizers for the rest of the book. The reader needs to know this because there are neither headings nor a table of contents. As Carl reads aloud the rest of the book he stops after each page and asks, "If you were going to give just this page a title, what would it be? I'm going to write down what you say so we have a record of exactly what kind of information we find out about frogs."

This record of student titles for each page functions like a table of contents for them. It also models a primitive form of notetaking to help them remember information. This is another good strategy used by readers of nonfiction. The students don't know it yet, but Carl plans to help them use these notes as they compile their own book about amphibians that answers their questions about frogs. For now, he tells the students, "We are going to read a lot of books about frogs as well as other amphibians, and this will help us remember what we read and where."

The conversational tone Carl uses during this guided reading lesson is suggestive of two friends discussing text. Carl is explicitly teaching without lecturing. Students are partners in the learning process and are encouraged and expected to join the conversation.

◆ ◆ ◆ Final Thoughts ◆ ◆ ◆

The children in these primary classrooms have learned to use talk as a learning tool. They know that talking with their teacher and fellow students can help them learn new concepts, clarify misunderstandings, and verify what they know. Not only do they know they can learn from others through talk, but they have also experienced the pleasure of contributing to other learners.

Through careful modeling and direct teaching experiences, these teachers helped the children learn the art of conversation. They helped children who tend to monopolize conversations understand that conversations involve hearing many voices—not just one. They have rehearsed with children reluctant to join in group discussions. Teachers and students have become collaborators in the learning process.

As the teachers at Central Primary School learned during their work together, the ability to talk and discuss freely leads to deep understandings. What worked for them in their adult class also worked well for children in their primary classrooms. The teachers explored how much they had learned from one another through the exchange of ideas, how new ideas had emerged, how misconceptions were clarified, and how nonthreatening the environment was. The teachers continued to meet periodically throughout the year; they considered James Britton's statement, "Writing floats on a sea of talk" (1970). They decided that they might amend the statement to say that *learning* floats on a sea of talk! In Chapter 7, which focuses on comprehension, you will see how talk is the critical vehicle for both learning and teaching comprehension.

Comprehension

Effective Teaching to Foster Comprehending Processes

The children in Kelly Berube's first-grade classroom are listening to her read the story *Tops & Bottoms* by Janet Stevens (Harcourt, 1995). In the story, a clever hare bargains with a lazy bear to grow food on the bear's land by agreeing to give the bear a part of each crop. But when the bear asks for the tops of the plants, the cagey hare plants seeds for foods that grow under the ground. The bear realizes he has been tricked, so next time he asks for the part of the crop that grows *under* the ground. While reading the story aloud, Kelly pauses to allow the children to talk about the story, guiding them to understand how the hare is tricking the lazy bear. During one pause, Abbey excitedly blurts out her new "ah-ha":

Abbey: Now I get it! The hare is tricking the bear so his family gets all of the food!

Kelly: You are right! That hare is tricking the bear. I wonder how he'll trick the bear this time. What do the rest of you think the hare might plant so that he gets all of the food? If the bear gets both the tops *and* the bottoms of the plant, what will be left for the hare?

Isaac: The middles!

Kelly: Oh, you think? [*Looking around at all the children*] Isaac thinks that the hare will grow plants that produce food in the middles. What could he grow that produces food in the middles?

Comprehending is something you do *while* you read so that you have comprehension *after* you read. Because comprehending (i.e., mental processes) during silent reading can't be seen or heard, interactive read-alouds externalize the comprehending for young children. Through pauses, wonderings, and questions, Kelly provides a concrete model of comprehending processes. Further, interactions with peers and the teacher give young learners opportunities to practice constructing the meaning of a story *during* the reading. In effect, interactive read-alouds help children develop the "habits of mind" needed for effective silent reading.

Interactive read-alouds provide the cornerstone for comprehension instruction in the preschool to second-grade years, before children can read literature independently. However, there are other methods teachers can use to foster these comprehending processes.

Overview of the Chapter

The purpose of this chapter is to show how comprehension instruction is fostered in preschool through second grade. Instruction is embedded in many activities and lessons throughout the day, and it is also fostered in vocabulary and fluency instruction. As Nell Duke and P. David Pearson (2002) suggest, effective comprehension instruction has many components. (See Figure 7.1.)

For instruction to be research-based, you have to keep the comprehension research in the back of your mind as you plan instruction. Therefore, this chapter begins with a brief review of the comprehension research as it relates to teaching preschool to second grade. In the preschool section you will see how a teacher lays the foundation for comprehending processes through interactive read-aloud. In the next section, on kindergarten, the teacher uses a very early guided reading text and much rich talk during the guided reading lesson to help young readers learn how to link their prior knowledge and experiences to more fully comprehend the setting and characters in the book. Then, a teacher's think-aloud in first grade models how a good reader "feels" the setting of a book to make it come alive. And finally, an extensive second-grade section shows how a teacher transitions young learners into reading nonfiction texts and having independent literature conversations.

Figure 7.1

Components of Effective Comprehension Instruction

- time spent reading
- experiences with a range of text genres
- experiences hearing and reading texts for authentic purposes
- vocabulary and concept development
- opportunities to build reading fluency
- opportunities to write texts for others to comprehend

Duke & Pearson, 2002, pp. 207–208.

Review of the Research on Comprehension

Here are the main points from the research to keep in the back of your mind as you organize for research-based comprehension instruction. Key questions to ask yourself as you use this research to guide instruction are highlighted for each point.

First, comprehension is an interaction between three main factors: the reader, the text, and the purpose for reading. (Irwin, 1991; RAND Reading

Reader, Text, and Purpose

Key questions for teachers:

- Who are my readers and what do they know?
- What are the demands of the particular text and will the demands match the readers' capabilities?
- Do the readers have a real and compelling reason to read, and have I taught them how to adjust their reading for specific purposes?

Study Group, 2002; Sweet & Snow, 2002) That is, the likelihood of particular readers reading and understanding particular texts depends on what background knowledge they have for the text topic, vocabulary, and genre, and their level of control over comprehending processes for that text. In addition, the purposes for which they are reading (e.g., for pleasure, for information) provide the motivation or incentive to comprehend.

Second, research indicates that good readers engage in a variety of comprehending processes leading to comprehension (Goodman & Goodman, 2004):

♦ activating background knowledge

♦ predicting

♦ using different comprehending processes on different types of text

♦ making connections

♦ imagining

♦ inferring

♦ monitoring, questioning, and repairing

♦ distinguishing important from less important ideas

♦ summarizing

♦ evaluating

♦ synthesizing

> ## Comprehending Processes
> ### Key questions for teachers:
> • Do I know what these comprehending processes look and feel like when I use them, so I can model them for my students?
> • Have I provided adequate support for students to learn how to use the comprehending processes in shared and read-aloud contexts before I require students to use them in guided and independent contexts?

These comprehending processes form an interactive network for thinking about and making meaning from print. They are the curriculum for reading comprehension instruction (Block & Pressley, 2003; Block et al., 2002; Duke & Pearson, 2002; Keene & Zimmerman, 1997; Pressley, 2000). While we may separate these processes to better understand them and to teach about them, good readers integrate these processes on the run. In this chapter you will see examples of teachers teaching these comprehension processes in interaction and individually.

Third, research indicates that children at the preschool to second-grade level need opportunities to listen to engaging texts and to experience models of comprehending processes in action (Rasinski, 2003). But they also need *explicit instruction* to learn how to use comprehending processes effectively on a variety of text types (Duke & Pearson, 2000; Pressley, 2000). An effective model for explicit comprehension instruction includes:

1. Explicit description of the strategy and when and how it should be used (as in a mini-lesson—the most teacher help).

2. Teacher and/or student modeling of the strategy in action (as in interactive read-aloud or shared reading).

3. Collaborative use of the strategy in action (as in shared reading or interactive read-aloud).

4. Guided practice using the strategy with gradual release of responsibility (as in guided reading).

5. Independent use of the strategy (Duke & Pearson, pp. 208-210) (as in independent literature conversations or independent reading—the least amount of teacher help).

> ### Explicit Comprehension Instruction
>
> **Key questions for teachers:**
>
> - Do I recognize the five "levels of support" when I see them?
>
> - Do the lessons or lesson sequences I design provide sufficient levels of support before I ask students to use strategies independently?
>
> - If students cannot use a strategy after I provide a lesson or lesson sequence, do I know to which level of support I need to return to provide the best level of help for my particular students at this particular time?

This model provides for a high level of teacher support or help at the beginning of the instructional sequence and gradually provides for more student initiative as students become more familiar with the use of these processes. Not all lessons need to have all five steps, but over time, several lessons may have decreasing levels of help to prepare students to use strategies independently.

In general, instruction at the preschool to second-grade levels involves first immersing young children in joyful experiences with books. Once they have experienced how to make meaning from books through conversations with caregivers, teachers, and peers, then comprehending processes can be brought out for overt examination (i.e., metacognitive awareness) through explicit instruction. However, comprehending processes are not ends in themselves; they are the means to an end. Therefore, explicit instruction is always embedded in purposes for reading. In other words, young children identify and learn how to control comprehending processes because they have a compelling reason to read and understand, and an urgent need to write and communicate.

Teaching to Foster Comprehension

In the next sections, you will see preschool through second-grade teachers using research-based teaching practices that ensure that children develop adequate comprehending strategies to read and write particular types of texts.

Comprehension Instruction in the PRESCHOOL

Laying the Foundation Through Joyful Experiences With Books and Rich Talk

In Angela Williams's preschool classroom the children are learning how to make sense of their world, and they are learning to use words, both oral and written, to convey meaning to others. Instruction in the preschool lays the groundwork for comprehending processes by immersing young children in joyful experiences with books and rich talk during many activities. During interactive read-aloud Angela supports the children as they learn to use the words and illustrations in the text to gain meaning from the text. The children participate in music and fingerplays that require careful listening and understanding in order to participate fully.

Fingerplays are a favorite activity in Angela's preschool class. Angela uses these simple fingerplays to determine if the children comprehend the words in the poems and songs well enough to follow the directions. She notices which children participate fully and which children simply watch others, then do what they see the other children doing.

The class enjoys songs with hand and body movements such as "Head, Shoulders, Knees, and Toes" and "The Hokey Pokey." While sitting on the carpet at center time the children participate in favorites such as "Where Is Thumbkin" and "Five Little Ducks."

Angela also has a collection of books that are simply songs written down. These books often include music and examples of movements. Class favorites include Raffi's *Wheels on the Bus* (Crown, 1988) and Michael Rosen's *We're Going on a Bear Hunt* (Aladdin, 2002). Once the children become familiar with the concept of movement based on the words of songs and poems, Angela asks them to invent movements to other familiar songs. She uses simple texts such as *The Bear Went Over the Mountain* by Rozanne Williams (Creative Teaching Press, 1994), *Baby Beluga* by Raffi (Crown, 1992), and *There's a Hole in My Pocket* by Akimi Gibson (Scholastic, 1994), which lend themselves to movement. Angela and the children discuss which movements might be appropriate based on the words in the texts.

The children in Angela's classroom are learning to listen carefully to the messages texts carry. They are learning that texts make sense and that their job as listeners is to interpret the words in the texts. These understandings will be reinforced throughout the preschool day.

Comprehension Instruction in KINDERGARTEN

Informal Talk During Guided Reading to Build Background Knowledge

As adults, we talk to others about interesting materials we have read, such as newspaper articles or novels. With our colleagues we discuss professional readings. Our talk helps us understand, learn different perspectives, and clarify our own thinking. The same holds true for the children we teach. The talk to foster comprehending processes may be either informal through book discussion (see for example, Cole, 2003; McLaughlin, 2003) or formal through explicit teaching (Cole, 2004; Owocki, 2003). The following is an example of how the informal talk during a kindergarten guided reading lesson fosters comprehending processes.

Anna, one of the authors of this book, recently taught a group of kindergartners during their very first guided reading lesson. She used the book *The Surprise* by Joy Cowley (Wright Group, 1988). The entire book contains only 16 words. The word *the* appears seven times, so there are really only eight different words in the book, each preceded by *the: dog, cat, rooster, frog, cake, flowers, balloons, surprise.* Gaining meaning from text with so few words may seem an impossible task. Illustrations in the book show the dog with an injured foot looking very sad. The cat, rooster, and frog gather the cake, flowers, and balloons to take to their friend the dog. The last page shows the three friends bringing the treats to the dog. The dog is clearly pleased and surprised.

Anna and the children looked at the illustrations together and talked about each one in turn. The children looked at the dog's injured foot and thought about what could have happened to cause the injury. The children discussed how the dog might feel and related experiences when they had been injured. They looked, talked, and wondered about the next seven pages. The children predicted the party to cheer up the dog and confirmed their prediction on the final page of the story.

In this discussion of the book and illustrations, Anna informally engaged the children in several comprehending processes used by good readers:

- They *made predictions* about the story (e.g., predicted a party to cheer up the dog).
- They *integrated their prior knowledge* (e.g., related experiences when they had been injured).
- Like good readers of fiction, they *attended closely to the setting and characters* (e.g., one child wondered if one of the other animals had caused the injury, and the party was a way to apologize).

The book introduction and discussion of the illustrations took ten minutes. It took the children a little more than a minute to read the story aloud to themselves. However, the informal talk between Anna and the children beforehand not only established critical background knowledge for the children to be able to read and comprehend a very simple story on a broader and more complex level, but it also implicitly engaged the children in comprehending processes.

Comprehension Instruction in FIRST GRADE

Modeling Through Teacher Think-Aloud

Teachers use think-alouds in many contexts to make comprehending processes external and concrete for young children. Think-alouds demonstrate to novice readers how a more expert reader interacts with a book to build comprehension while reading. Let's visit Susan Lacy's first-grade class again. In the following think-aloud example, Susan demonstrates how a reader might imagine or visualize as she reads in order to really "feel" the setting of the book *Scruffy: A Wolf Finds His Place in the Pack* by Jim Brandenburg (Walker, 1996):

Susan: Br-r-r, as I look at this page I am imagining how cold the snow feels, and how if I were there, I would be bundled up in my warmest jacket and snow pants. I would have my hood up and tied tightly under my chin because the wind is blowing so hard it almost knocks me over. And I can imagine how the cold freezes the tip of my nose and my cheeks. Good readers imagine themselves in the book they are reading, and they feel, hear, and see what's happening. That's how you make a book come alive.

Susan used the pictures to demonstrate how she imagined the arctic snow and wind would feel. As she continued through the book she invited students to talk with one another about what they saw, heard, or felt (collaborative use of the strategy of *imagining*). Susan will provide support for students to learn how to imagine during many read-alouds and shared reading lessons during the year. Eventually, she will choose books for each guided reading group that allows students to practice imagining or using their senses as they read in a guided reading context. Finally, at the end of the year, Susan will transition some students into independent literature conversations where she will prompt students to share their sensory perceptions with one another.

Using illustrations is a good way to begin teaching young children about how readers imagine, visualize, or feel as they engage all their senses during reading. Illustrations provide a concrete segue into the more complex imagining needed as readers respond to words.

You can use think-aloud to model comprehending processes during read-alouds, shared reading, or guided reading. Teacher modeling through think-aloud is most effective when it is explicit, leaving the student to intuit or infer little about the comprehending process being modeled and its application (Duke & Pearson, 2002). Think-aloud as an instructional device provides a high level of support (i.e., explicit description of strategy or teacher modeling). It is followed up with opportunities for students to use the strategy modeled by the teacher in collaboration with others and in guided reading contexts. In other words, think-aloud is not sufficient on its own.

Comprehension Instruction in SECOND GRADE

Nonfiction Guided Reading and Independent Literature Conversations

Second graders are usually "transitional" readers transitioning to greater independence in silent reading. For that reason, second grade is often the time when young readers begin to read nonfiction independently and discuss literature in small groups. In this section you will find examples of comprehension instruction in these two new areas: nonfiction reading and literature discussions.

Nonfiction Guided Reading

Comprehending nonfiction text places demands on novice readers, very different from those required by fiction reading. For one, fiction is usually organized in beginning-to-end order for it to follow a story sequence. You have to read it in order to make sense of it. However, nonfiction texts usually contain special features and organizational structures that allow the author to convey information in a variety of ways: through sidebars, subsections, and headings, through a glossary or index, etc. You can read these features in any order and still make sense of the text (Kristo & Bamford, 2004). Novice nonfiction readers usually need explicit instruction in how to recognize and use nonfiction features and organizational devices.

While preschool to second-grade teachers often read aloud or share text to develop young readers' "ears" for the features and organizational structures of nonfiction, young learners often begin reading nonfiction for themselves toward the end of first grade and into second grade. In the following example, second-grade teacher Carl Porter introduces a guided reading group to a particular type of nonfiction text. Carl has already used read-aloud and shared reading to focus on nonfiction (see Chapter 6), and he usually introduces nonfiction reading and writing in conjunction with a particular science unit. He tries to find an appropriate-level nonfiction text on that same subject for each guided reading group so they have prior knowledge about the topic and are able to transition to reading nonfiction for themselves without a heavy content load.

In this example, Carl met with Spencer, Miranda, and Nathan. Though it was January, these second graders were just beginning to read second-grade-level texts. Carl chose a nonfiction book that he thought might be a bit below their fiction reading level. That way the text itself would be easier for them to read, and they could focus just on the new strategy of using organizational devices to read for information. In addition, reading nonfiction text with understanding is in large part dependent on what you already know about the topic. For example, we educators might have difficulty reading a journal for chemical engineers because we lack the background knowledge and vocabulary to understand the subject. The book Carl chose for Spencer, Miranda, and Nathan was on a topic they had prior knowledge of from their science unit—frogs.

Specifically, Carl chose Angela Royston's book *Frog*, from the See How They Grow series (Lodestar Books, 1991). The book is an easy-to-follow life-cycle book that combines photographs and illustrations to show the life cycle of a frog, from frog spawn to year-old frog. It has simple headings on each two-page layout, and the text is really like a long caption for each photograph or illustration. This is a good book on which to begin practicing nonfiction comprehension strategies because it has no sidebars, insets, or complex captions or pictures competing for the novice reader's attention.

Carl's students have been working with comprehension strategies all year. They use a simple list (see Figure 7.2) to remind themselves how readers think while they are reading. The list is in student language, but you will recognize the comprehending processes from Chapter 2 and the sidebar at the beginning of this chapter (Block & Pressley, 2003; Duke & Pearson, 2002; Duffy, 2003; Kristo & Bamford, 2004; Pearson et al., 1992).

For this lesson Carl focused on the last strategy listed: *Pay attention to the type of text you are reading, fiction or nonfiction. This helps you read better for understanding and information.* Carl began his guided reading lesson with Spencer, Miranda, and Nathan by reviewing the comprehending processes. Next he introduced the students to the idea that paying attention to the way a nonfiction book is organized is one way good readers can help themselves read better for information. The students have already examined survey books that provide a survey of many facts about a topic. They should be ready to recognize that a life-cycle book is not a survey but is organized chronologically around just one type of fact, the life cycle of a frog.

Figure 7.2

Thinking While You Read

1. Use what you know to help you think about the text, even before you start reading.

2. Make predictions about what might come next and then read to see if it happens.

3. Make connections **in** the text, **between** texts, and **with yourself**.

4. Imagine what is happening: see, hear, smell, taste, and feel what the author is telling you. You should feel like you are **in** the book.

5. Use clues to figure things out, even when the author does not say it right out. Use what you already know as well as hints in the text.

6. Listen to yourself and make sure that what you are reading makes sense. If it doesn't, go back and fix it.

7. Pay attention to the most important ideas, and don't mix them up with little details.

8. Make judgments about what the author is saying. Is it right? Is it true?

9. Pay attention to the type of text you are reading, fiction or nonfiction. This helps you read better for understanding and information.

Then, Carl set a purpose for their reading. Typically, Carl does not grill students when they finish reading to find out if they *comprehended*. Instead, he tries to set a purpose for reading that will keep the students interested and tuned in to *comprehending*. Each of the students in this group is to discover at least one new thing about frogs after reading the book to add to their science chart. If they can't, Carl will be worried about their comprehending. In addition, he planned to listen to each of them read *Frog* the next day and take a running record. Let's tune in to Carl's lesson:

Carl: Today I have a nonfiction book about frogs for us to read to see if we can find out anything new about this topic we are studying. [*Holding up the text for students to see.*] It is called *Frog*. It's from a series called See How They Grow, which has a lot of books about animals and how they grow from babies into adults. [*Pointing to the chart on the board behind him as a reminder for them to use the comprehending processes.*] Okay, use what you know to predict what this book will be about.

Nathan: It's going to be about how frogs grow.

Carl: Spencer and Miranda, do you agree? [*Students nod heads in agreement.*]

Carl: So, you know from the title that this is a book just about how frogs grow. What books can you make a connection to?

Spencer: Hey—it's like that book you read to us today!

Carl had read *All About Frogs* by Jim Arnosky (Scholastic, 2002) to the class as an example of a survey-type nonfiction text. Survey texts tell the reader lots of facts about a topic. Now, Carl has to make sure the students don't mistake a survey-type organizational pattern with a life-cycle organizational pattern.

Carl: Spencer, in what way is it like the book I read to you today?

Spencer: It's about frogs.

Carl: Yes, that is true. But there is one way that this book is not like *All About Frogs*—it is organized differently. Remember, survey books tell you a lot of facts about a topic. This book is not going to survey a lot of facts; it is going to tell you a lot about just one fact. What is that fact?

Miranda: How frogs grow.

Carl: Yeah! It's just about how frogs grow. I chose it for you because it is like lots of books that are about how things grow. And you can use how this book is organized to help understand the information. Remember, one of your strategies [*turning to chart and gesturing to no. 9*] is *Pay attention to the type of text you are reading, fiction or nonfiction. This helps you read better for understanding and information.* Can you guess how a book about the life cycle of a frog will be organized?

Nathan: Maybe it's organized by like how frogs grow—from tadpoles to big frogs?

Carl: That would make sense, and I already told you that it is like a lot of other books in the series that tell how an animal grows from the baby stage into adulthood. Let's just look at the pictures and read the headings and see if Nathan is right. [*Hands students each a book to look through.*] Remember, don't start reading; just read the headings and look at the pictures.

[*Nathan does not really read the headings; he quickly turns pages while the other two do a more thorough examination.*]

Nathan: I know! I know! I was right! It's organized by how frogs grow.

Carl: Let's wait and see what Spencer and Miranda think.

Miranda: Yup. It's by how frogs grow. [*Spencer nods in agreement.*]

Carl: What exactly are the clues that this is organized around changes in a frog's growth?

Nathan: The pictures show how the frog grows.

Carl: Are there any other hints? How about the headings—they always give a reader good clues about organization.

Miranda: It's like, [*She reads headings as she flips pages*] "Growing in jelly," then, "Just hatched," and then "Tadpole."

Carl: Okay, so the headings kind of sum up each stage in the frog's growth. You all did an excellent job figuring out this book's organization. It is called a life cycle–type nonfiction book because it tells about the frog's growth from egg to frog. Both the pictures and the headings give you clues about how the book is organized. If you know how the book is organized, then you can predict or be ready for what might come next in the life cycle. And you can use the stages of growth to remember the information.

There was just one tricky place on page 6 for me. I don't want you to get tricked. Notice the picture of the frog's eggs on this page. I would have just called them eggs, but the author uses the term *frog spawn*. *Spawn* means a mass of eggs, and that is certainly a mass of eggs. Have you ever seen frog spawn in a pond or lake? [*It is common for nonfiction books to have specialized vocabulary, or Tier Three words. You may need to specifically introduce those words to students before they read.*]

[*Students share their experiences with frog eggs.*]

Carl: I think you are ready to try reading this. Read to see if your predictions about what will happen in this life-cycle book are correct. And remember, listen to yourself when you are reading, and if it doesn't make sense, go back and fix it. And, if you come to a hard word, what will you try?

Spencer: First read the sentence again and see if you can think of a word that would make sense. Then look at the word and see what word parts you know.

Carl: Perfect! Be ready to share any new things you learned about the frog life cycle when you finish. Remember, you are going to write one new fact about frogs on the science chart. Go ahead and read.

After the students finished reading and talking about one new thing they learned, Carl reviewed the concept that how a book is organized helps you read for and remember important information. Carl will continue introducing nonfiction features and organizational structures during a monthlong unit integrating reading/language arts and the science topic of amphibians. This is one case in which the five levels of support outlined in the model of comprehension instruction will be spread out over a very long time before students will be able to read nonfiction text without the support of read-aloud, shared reading, think-aloud, and guided reading experiences. Eventually, Carl's students will create their own book about amphibians to show not only what they know about the topic, but also what they know about nonfiction text features and organizational structures.

Independent Literature Conversations

Independent literature conversations are another way to foster comprehension in a classroom with transitional readers. Reading and talking about books that interest them turns students on to reading (motivation!); consequently, they read more (extended practice), which research indicates is related to increases in vocabulary and fluency as well as comprehension (Duke & Pearson, 2002; Graves & Watts-Taffe, 2002; Samuels, 2002).

However, the students in Carl's second-grade class did not come naturally to talking about books. They learned how to do it with careful step-by-step preparation (Cole, 2003). First, Carl introduced the students to the workings of effective conversation. They observed conversations, made lists of factors that contribute to effective conversation, and practiced conversations. They developed an ongoing "conversations tips" chart.

Second, the students learned how to have conversations specifically about the books Carl read aloud to them. Carl kept it simple. All conversations about books started with an "I wonder." Wondering or questioning the text is the foundation of all the comprehension processes (Cole, 2003, p. 25). Using read-alouds, Carl modeled many aspects of text about which a reader might wonder:

- ◆ a character's intent
- ◆ the author's intent
- ◆ a word choice or meaning of a word
- ◆ how an author thinks up ideas
- ◆ other points of view besides the one portrayed in a particular book
- ◆ how illustrations or photographs were chosen to illustrate a book

- how a book connects to life or another book
- whether or not a book is fact or fiction
- whether or not a story could really happen
- why an author chose to end a story in a particular way
- why a nonfiction writer decided to structure a book one way and not another

These are just a sample of the many ways readers might wonder about a text. Carl discovered that wondering was an excellent way to open conversations about both fiction and nonfiction text. He felt the simple device fostered complex levels of comprehension, such as analysis, evaluation, imagining, and making connections, much better than traditional comprehension questions. By listening to children's wonderings, Carl was able to tell the extent to which they really understood a text.

Third, Carl taught students how to take notes about their "I wonder" statements using sticky notes or a reading journal during read-aloud and guided reading. These notes helped students to notice and listen to their thinking as they read. This is a learned comprehension process. Students may read the words but may not really "hear" what they are reading and thinking. Notes the students made functioned like the notes many of us have written in the margins of texts we are reading for our own book discussions. They are short memory jogs, helpful when you begin talking about a book with others. Ardith Cole in her book *Knee to Knee, Eye to Eye*, (2003), has this to say about the importance of notes and notetaking:

> **A student's self-generated thoughts on texts are often more revealing than the overused fill-in-someone-else's-blank workbook pages and blackline masters. Logged notes also become a first step in the necessary skill of notetaking and they lay a concrete trail for the comprehension strategy of referencing previous information for evidence—all of which needs to be modeled, modeled, modeled. (p. 78)**

Finally, Carl taught his students how to have conversations with one other person during and after read-alouds and during guided reading. The students practiced using their "I wonder" notes and followed their conversation tips with help from Carl. Eventually, the students worked in groups of three to converse about read-alouds and guided reading text.

As students became more independent in holding conversations and as they began reading longer books, Carl transitioned students into independent literature conversation groups. He presented a variety of interesting books at the students' reading levels, let them choose the books they wanted to read, and then placed those reading the same book in conversation groups of no more than three. Ardith Cole (2003, p. 71) suggests that three is the optimal number for collaborative conversation groups.

Carl met with each small group first to explain that they would be reading their books independently and holding conversations on their own. They would be deciding on how much to read and when to meet to talk about their books. Occasionally, Carl asked students to evaluate their independent conversations using a checklist that included items about how the group worked together, how well prepared they were when they met, how well they conversed, and how well they made connections with life, with themselves, and with other texts.

Today, Carl is going to listen in on a literature conversation that Mia, Keisha, and Kate are having. He doesn't think it is necessary to monitor every single conversation that literature groups are having. However, he knows that his second graders are just learning how to read and converse independently, and he wants to check in regularly to see if they need help. He tries to check in on one literature conversation each day. Mia, Keisha, and Kate are reading *The Great Escape* by Susan Akass (2000) from a series of short chapter books for second graders published by Rigby. In the story, a young girl finally gets a hamster of her own. When the hamster disappears one day, the family cat is the prime suspect. Mia, Keisha, and Kate have just finished Chapter 2, "Tiger Waits," in which the hamster has disappeared, and the cat's footprints lead up the stairs to where the hamster's cage lies in pieces.

Mia: I wonder where the cat went? Like, if it ate the hamster, where is it?

Keisha: She didn't look in the closet. I bet the cat went in the closet chasing the hamster. See? It says she looked [*reading from the text*] "under the bed, under the dresser, in her toy box." But, she never looked in her closet.

Kate: Yeah, but the cat was back at supper time. Remember, the dad asked Catherine to feed it and she started crying.

Mia: How come she didn't tell her dad and mom right away that the hamster was gone?

Keisha: I'd get another hamster if my mom said she'd get me one.

Mia: Well, I wouldn't 'cause it wouldn't be the same as Magic.

Keisha: Yeah, but it'd be a hamster!

Kate: But we don't even know if the hamster really got eaten by the cat yet. Maybe it didn't!

Carl was pleased that the girls were all wondering about aspects of the text by going back into the text to check details that support their points with evidence. They sometimes had a little trouble sustaining conversations because one of them would take a stance and not give up, as Keisha and Mia seemed to be doing about whether or not it was appropriate to accept the mom's offer to get another hamster. Carl made a mental note to bring up the issue of what to do in a group if members disagreed and could not seem to stop arguing. It would be another topic for the conversations tips chart. For now, he suggested that the girls follow up on Kate's point and read some more to find out if the cat really did eat the hamster.

♦ ♦ ♦ Final Thoughts ♦ ♦ ♦

The children in these classrooms are learning about comprehending processes through exploration, observation, talk, and interactions with others, just as they have done from birth. While teachers continue to foster this learning, they also help children add reading and writing to their repertoires. They use authentic contexts for reading and writing and stress meaning-making throughout lessons.

Comprehension strategies must be explicitly taught, but strategies are best taught in meaningful contexts so children have a real reason to use them. Comprehension worksheets and isolated drills do not always transfer to actual reading and writing. By showing children authentic reasons for reading and writing, teachers keep them engaged in literacy learning and actively comprehending. In Chapter 8, on vocabulary, you will find examples for teaching vocabulary in a variety of instructional contexts found in preschool to second grade.

CHAPTER 8

Vocabulary

Effective Teaching to Foster Vocabulary Development

It is 8 A.M. in Angela Payne's preschool classroom. "Look at me," says Jonathan, "I'm a doctor!" Jonathan is wearing a long white smock and has a toy stethoscope around his neck. The housekeeping area of the preschool classroom has been transformed into a hospital. At a small bed in the corner, a child pretending to be a nurse is examining a doll. Two children are at the writing center making signs for the hospital.

At the block center, three children are building a bridge. There is a great deal of lively conversation as the bridge tumbles down and efforts are made to reconstruct a more sturdy bridge. After one unsuccessful attempt, Sarah shouts at Charlie, "You made it fall again!" Charlie bursts into tears. Angela takes the children aside. "Take a deep breath," she says, "and use your words to tell me what happened."

The children explain that they were trying to build a bridge and when Charlie placed his block on top, the bridge fell. "I know that is frustrating," Angela says, "but shouting at Charlie didn't fix the bridge. It only made Charlie sad." Angela then engages the children in a conversation about the bridge, why they think it fell, and how it might be fixed. They role-play how they could have responded to the situation in a more positive way. Two more attempts result in a bridge strong enough to hold toy cars. There are smiles all around. And through this rich conversation, Angela is helping to develop these preschoolers' vocabularies.

Overview of the Chapter

This chapter shows how read-alouds and shared reading of children's litera-ture provide the springboards for vocabulary instruction. Vocabulary development also happens easily and naturally as a part of a lesson on com-prehension or as part of an interactive writing lesson fostering early print skills. You will also see how vitally important conversation is for teaching vocabulary in the primary grades.

In the preschool section, we visit a classroom in which a teacher fosters both concept and vocabulary development through conversations around work centers. In the next section on kindergarten, you will see how the teacher adapts the six-step process proposed by Beck et al. (2002) for teach-ing vocabulary words as part of her interactive writing. Then, an interactive read-aloud paired with interactive writing is the context for an example of concept and vocabulary development in first grade. And finally, in a second-grade classroom, nonfiction literature and content area studies provide opportunities for vocabulary development. But first, we provide a short review of important points from the research to remember about vocabulary instruction.

Review of Research on Vocabulary

Summarized here are three main points from the research on vocabulary instruction presented in Chapter 3. Once again, we've included questions teachers can ask themselves as they reflect on the research related to teaching.

1. Research suggests that concept-based vocabulary instruction has the most lasting impact on student learning (Allen, 1999; Thompkins & Blanchfield, 2004) because vocabulary words are concepts. To connect concepts with vocabulary instruction teachers should teach

    • new concepts and new vocabulary together. For example, teach both the concept and the word for *crowded*.

    • new words for existing concepts. For example, teach the new words *launder*, *cleanse*, or *bathe* and relate them to the known word *wash*.

    • so that students relate known words to new concepts. For example, if students know what a *cup* for milk is, then teach the new concept of *cupping* hands to drink water or hoist a friend over a fence.

    • so that students relate known words to known concepts. For example, teach so that students learn that *dog* can refer not only to the family pet, but also to a family of wild animals.

2. Tier Two words should be the focus for most vocabulary instruction. They are words for abstract concepts (e.g., *coincidence*, *absurd*, *fortunate*), as opposed to words for more concrete concepts and actions, like *baby*, *clock*, or *run*.

Connecting Concepts With Vocabulary During Instruction

Key questions for teachers:

• Am I connecting concepts with vocabulary during instruction?

• Am I using the various methods to make these connections?

Making Word Choices for Vocabulary Instruction

Key questions for teachers:

• How generally useful is the word? Is it a word that students are likely to meet often in other texts? Will it be of use to students in describing their own experiences?

• How does the word relate to other words, to ideas that students know or have been learning? Does it directly relate to some topic of study in the classroom? Or might it add a dimension to ideas that have been developed?

• What does the word bring to the text or situation? What role does the word play in communicating the meaning of the context in which it is used?

Beck et al., 2002.

However, there is no formula for selecting grade-appropriate words for vocabulary instruction. As long as a word can be explained so young children can understand, it is an appropriate word to teach (Beck et al., 2002).

3. And finally, Michael Graves and Susan Watts-Taffe (2002) recommend a four-part program to teach vocabulary:

Part 1: Wide Reading. Choose books for read-aloud and shared reading from a wide variety of high-quality children's literature and big books.

Part 2: Teaching Individual Words. Teach two or three individual words each day. Follow a six-step sequence such as 1) remind children of the context for the word in the book, 2) ask the children to say the word aloud, 3) explain the meaning of the word, 4) provide examples of other contexts in which the word might be used, 5) ask children to use the word themselves, and 6) ask children to say the word again. (This six-step framework for teaching individual words comes from Beck et al., 2002.)

Part 3: Teaching Word-Learning Strategies. Explicitly teach children specific strategies to figure out the meaning of new words.

Part 4: Fostering Word Consciousness. Create a classroom context in which awareness of and interest in words is aroused (Graves & Watts-Taffe, 2002).

A Four-Part Program for Vocabulary Instruction

Key questions for teachers:

- Are there many opportunities for students to listen to and read books in my classroom?

- Am I teaching two to three new vocabulary words daily?

- Am I teaching students how to figure out new vocabulary on their own?

- Am I creating a classroom context in which awareness of and interest in words is fostered?

Teaching to Foster Vocabulary Development

In the following classroom examples, you will see how teachers use conversations to naturally foster children's vocabularies in developmentally appropriate ways.

Vocabulary Development in PRESCHOOL

Centers That Foster Word Consciousness

Word learning naturally permeates the day in Angela Payne's preschool classroom. Through rich conversations about activities in learning centers, daily special events, and read-alouds, children hear and use many new words and concepts. The first hour of the day is spent in free-choice centers such as those described in the opening vignette of the chapter. These centers allow time for everyone to arrive and adjust to the preschool environment. The hour also provides time for brief conversations between the teacher and the caregivers who drop off the children. While the activities at the centers are free choice, a great deal of learning is taking place.

The children at the hospital center are using new vocabulary learned the day before. While they are not yet reading and writing these words, the words will become a part of their speaking and listening vocabularies. Their new understandings will help with the comprehension of stories read aloud, and with future writing. Two days ago the class had engaged in an interactive read-aloud of the story *Curious George Goes to the Hospital* by Margaret and H. A. Rey (Houghton Mifflin, 1966). A local pediatrician visited the same day. By turning the housekeeping center into a hospital, Angela is encouraging the children to role-play using their new understandings of the role of doctors and nurses. She also listens carefully for use of new vocabulary during the role-play activity. She is pleased that Maria and Charlotte chose to make signs. They wrote "kwt!!! I m sk" (Quiet! I am sick). The girls placed their sign at the entrance to the hospital.

At the block center, Angela encouraged Charlie and Sarah to use words to convey their feelings. She also used the word *frustrated* to describe what the children were feeling. She made a mental note to read *When Sophie Gets Angry—Very, Very Angry* by Molly Bang (Blue Sky Press, 1999) aloud the following day to help the children further explore concepts and words for anger and frustration.

In the preschool classroom, conversations about activities, events, and books the children have experienced form the foundation for rich concept-based vocabulary development. Conversation continues to form the foundation for vocabulary instruction in kindergarten.

Vocabulary Development in KINDERGARTEN

Fostering Word Awareness During Interactive Writing

Most of the kindergartners in Donna Cain's classroom are not yet writing on their own. They must learn not only to write letters and words but also to understand how to compose coherent text. In order to help children understand the writing process, Donna begins interactive writing during the first week of school. She knows that interactive writing makes the writing process visible to the children and offers them the support they will need to construct meaningful messages. During an interactive writing lesson, the children learn to write for an authentic purpose, negotiate a text, share the pen with the teachers to write the message, and reread often. Conversation is key to the process for both the teacher and the children (McCarrier, Pinnell, & Fountas, 2000).

In this lesson, Donna's class recalls the morning read-aloud of Kevin Henkes's charming book *Wemberly Worried* (Greenwillow, 2000). (You read how Donna introduced the book during shared reading with her kindergartners in Chapter 6.) Now, she uses it as a springboard for authentic writing and for deepening the children's understanding of the Tier Two word *worry*. During this lesson, Donna reinforces much literacy learning besides vocabulary. Effective teaching and learning in the early grades often integrates many literacy concepts, skills, and strategies when reading and writing for authentic purposes. And notice as you read the lesson how the teaching feels like a conversation. Donna uses a variation on the six-step sequence developed by Beck et al. (2002) for teaching individual words.

Donna: This morning we read a story about a mouse named Wemberly and how much she worried. She was especially worried about going to school for the first time. We were all glad that Wemberly found a friend at school and didn't need to worry so much. Several of you told me that you were worried about some things at school too.

> **Reminds children of the context in the book for the word *worry* and its meaning. Then reminds children of other contexts in which the word might be used by using their examples from the morning discussion. (Steps 1 and 5)**

Jim: I was worried about riding the school bus.

Cindy: I didn't think I'd be able to find our room.

Tyrell: The big kids on the bus made me worry.

Donna: That's right! I remember now. Several of you were worried about the bus. Julie was worried about not finding our classroom. Help me remember what else you were worried about.

[Several children mention being lost, not having friends, and losing their lunch money or other cafeteria issues.]

Donna: Thank you for helping me remember. I would like for us to remember the things our class is worried about. Then we can decide some things to do so we won't need to worry so much. One way to remember things is to write a list. Yesterday I went to the grocery store and I made a list to take with me. I brought my list to show you. I wrote: *milk, bread, spaghetti, lettuce, carrots, tomatoes, cheese.*

New Essentials for Teaching Reading in PreK–2

Donna: When I go to the store, I want to get everything I need so I can make dinner for my family, so I make a list to help me remember what I need. Would it help if we make a list of all of the things we're worried about? Then we can look at our list and decide what to do to help each other.

Deepens children's understanding of the concept *worry* by creating a list that can be read and reread and used to make decisions. (Step 4)

[Donna sits at an easel with large sheets of paper attached. She engages the children in conversation about what a list looks like. The children decide to give their list the title "Things We Worry About." Donna writes the title at the top of the chart paper. Then she points to each word and reads it to the children. She invites the children to say the words with her while she points.]

Donna: Now that we have our title, let's think about the first thing we want to write on the list.

Jim: I worry about the bus. My mom said to remember my bus number. What if I forget?

Brenda: There are lots of big kids on my bus and they are loud.

Rosita: I'm worried that I might get lost and no one will find me.

Kayla: The bus might leave me at school. I don't want to sleep here!

Donna: It sounds like lots of you worry about the bus. Brenda worries about the loud voices, and Kayla and Tony are worried that the bus might leave them. Do we need to put the bus on our list of things we worry about?

Figure 8.1

Things We Worry About

1. the Bus
2. Getting lost
3. Big Kids
4. the Cafeteria

[The children all agree that the bus should be on the list, and Donna reminds the children that list items need contain only one or two words as reminders. The children decide that they will only need to write the bus. The rest of the lesson now focuses on hearing and recording sounds in the words and learning sight words.]

When the children finish their list (see Figure 8.1) using interactive writing and help from Donna, they proudly hang it on the wall so they can revisit it the next day. They will continue to add worries to the list, as well as solutions. In this way Donna is teaching many early literacy concepts and skills, and vocabulary development is naturally integrated. By keeping the list of worries on the wall and adding to it, the concept *worry* and the word *worry* are reinforced.

Shared Reading as a Springboard for Vocabulary Development

In the primary grades, read-alouds and shared reading provide the "wide-reading" portion of the four-part vocabulary program recommended by Graves and Watts-Taffe. Kelly Berube spends the first month of school doing lots of shared reading and interactive writing with her first graders. She says that when she starts guided reading groups in October, most children will have gained at least one or two text levels from the beginning of the year. In this lesson, Kelly used a big book of *Rosie's Walk* by Pat Hutchins (Simon & Schuster, 1968) to help develop her students' understanding and use of prepositions. *Rosie's Walk* is an old book, but it is still a favorite. In the book, Rosie the hen goes for a walk

> **across the yard**
> **around the pond**
> **over the haystack**
> **past the mill**
> **through the fence**
> **under the beehives**
> **and got back in time for dinner.**

To the slapstick amusement of young readers, a fox stalks the nonchalant Rosie relentlessly as she walks around the farm. Large illustrations, often covering the page, show the unfortunate fox encountering one mishap after another as he attempts to grab Rosie as she strolls along, completely oblivious to the danger that lurks behind her. The simple story and delightful illustrations provide many opportunities for students and teacher to interact.

Kelly used the book to teach position words (e.g., *in, on, over, under*) in a concrete way. She calls them "position words" rather than prepositions to make them more understandable to first graders. While they are not Tier Two words, prepositions represent abstract concepts and are often difficult for young readers and writers to grasp. In addition, the written form of many prepositions, such as *on, of,* and *off,* share visual similarities and are easily confused by young readers. Therefore, it pays to do a lesson on prepositions that integrates both concept development and an opportunity for children to develop sight recognition of the words for reading and writing.

Kelly gathered the children on the rug, seated herself by the easel with the closed big book, pointer in hand.

Kelly: Boys and girls, this is a story about a hen that takes a walk around the farm. But, unbeknownst to her, a hungry fox is following her, waiting for a chance to grab a chicken dinner. It's called *Rosie's Walk*, and it was written by Pat Hutchins. Look at the cover of the book. What do you see?

[The children and Kelly talk about the cover illustration. Kelly blends her observations with the children's and helps them notice and name the henhouse and the windmill in the background.]

The first page sets the stage for the story. The two-page illustration shows a high-stepping Rosie beginning her walk while the hungry fox sneaks out from under the henhouse, with his tongue hanging out in anticipation of a tasty chicken dinner.

Kelly: [*Turns to the first page of the story and points and reads*] "Rosie the hen went for a walk."

Kelly: Oh, no! What do you see sneaking out from under the henhouse? [*She pauses to let the children interact. Then she turns to the next page. The children immediately react as the illustration shows Rosie blissfully unaware, walking across the yard, with the fox about to pounce on her. Kelly points and reads, "across the yard."*]

Kelly: Uh-oh! Do you think the fox will get her? [*The children excitedly make their predictions. They do not notice the rake lying on the ground with its tines in the air. She turns to the next page. The children laugh with delight. The fox has missed Rosie and pounced on the upturned tines of the rake. The rake hits him in the head. It is perfect slapstick humor for six-year-olds.*]

Kelly: What happened here? [*The children are fully engaged in the story and clamor to tell what has happened. She turns to the next page. The children excitedly exclaim as they see the fox about to pounce on Rosie again as she walks "around the pond."*]

Kelly: Is the fox going to get her this time? [*Some children catch on immediately and predict the fox will land in the pond.*]

The next page shows the fox plunging into the pond as Rosie walks calmly on. And so the story goes, each page creating suspense, with the following page showing the fox meeting a mishap as Rosie walks on, completely undeterred.

For the first reading, Kelly lets the children delight in the story, talking and interacting about the illustrations as they slowly make their way through the book. Then she rereads the book again a little faster with the children chiming in on the words. Finally, on the third reading of the book, she brings the children's attention to the position words.

In this lesson Kelly adapted Beck, McKeown, and Kucan's (2002) six-step framework for teaching individual vocabulary words. Notice how naturally Kelly embeds this framework for teaching vocabulary into her conversation and the activities. Kelly builds in all the steps in the framework, but she does it over several days and activities. It is a good example of how a research-based framework can be used as a guide for instruction and need not be implemented in a rigid, lockstep manner.

several sittings

Kelly: In this book there are a lot of words used to explain where Rosie was walking. I call them position words because they tell what position you are in as you do something. [*As Kelly turns the pages and reads the book again, she highlights and discusses each position word. Then she guides students as they demonstrate the action in the room.*] On the first page, Rosie is walking *across* the yard. Mackenzie, can you stand up and walk *across* the room for us?

> **Reminds children of context for words in the book. Then explains the meaning of the word. (Steps 1 and 3)**

> **Concrete examples of another context in which the word can be used. (Step 4)**

Kelly: On the next page Rosie is walking *around* the pond. Dana, you stand up and walk *around* us on the rug.

[*When Kelly finishes this reading of the book with the children demonstrating each position word, she then makes a proposal:*]

Kelly: Let's make our own book about us walking on the playground using these position words. I'll take your picture doing the action, and we'll make our own big book. First, think what position word you would like to show out on the playground—let's see—someone could walk *under* the slide. Someone could walk *across* the playground. What else could someone do? [*Most children quickly suggest a position word, and they all try to do something different.*]

> **Asks children to use the word themselves. (Step 5)**

Kelly and the children went out to the playground, and Kelly took pictures using a digital camera. She printed out the children's pictures after school. The next day they made their own big book, *We Play on the Playground,* using interactive writing. Each position word was written in a different color as a way to emphasize and highlight it. (Step 6: The children said the position words many times to reinforce the phonological representation.) The children read and reread their jointly constructed writing many

New Essentials for Teaching Reading in PreK–2

times as they completed their sentences and later when they read their big book during shared reading or independently. Finally, each position word went on the word wall for the children to reference in their own writing. (Steps 5 and 6: Vocabulary words are revisited many times as children use them in their reading and writing.)

In this activity, sparked by a shared reading of *Rosie's Walk*, Kelly has helped her students understand through concrete actions both the concepts and words for common prepositions. In the next example, a second-grade teacher, Carl Porter, also uses a read-aloud as a springboard for teaching vocabulary, as well as a concept. It was part of an integrated language arts and science unit.

Vocabulary Development in SECOND GRADE

Learning Words as Part of Content Area Studies

In chapters 6 and 7, we visited Carl Porter and his second-grade students. In Chapter 6, we saw how Carl used the book *All About Frogs* by Jim Arnosky (Scholastic, 2002) with a guided reading group to introduce the genre of survey-type nonfiction. In Chapter 7, he used the book *Frog* by Angela Royston from the Dorling Kindersley See How They Grow series to focus on recognizing and using nonfiction text structures to help comprehension. Today, he will again use the book *All About Frogs* with another group of students to integrate a vocabulary lesson.

First Lesson: Using the Six-Step Framework

Carl read the book aloud, reminding his students about the features of a nonfiction survey-type text. He and the students discussed new facts they were learning about frogs. As Carl closed the book, he began using Beck, McKeown, and Kucan's (2002) six-step framework for teaching the Tier Two word *survey*. In this example, Carl implemented the framework roughly in order. Carl

1. **contextualized the word.** "The book I read to you today was a nonfiction book organized as a *survey* of many facts about frogs."

2. **asked students to say the word aloud.** "Please say the word *survey* with me."

3. **explained the meaning of the word.** "Remember, I said a *survey* is a general overview of a lot of information. It would not be a survey if the book had told you a lot about just one aspect of frogs. For example, if the book told you just about how frogs are born and grow, this would

not be a survey. It would be a book with a lot of detail about just one little aspect of frogs. In *All About Frogs* you found out how frogs are born and grow, but you also found out about where frogs live, what they eat, and how many kinds of frogs there are. It was a survey of many facts about frogs."

4. **gave examples of the word used in other contexts.** "You can also use the word *survey* in other ways, but it always means a general overview. For example, people survey their land to determine its general location, shape, and boundaries and to map it. People also survey other people to find out in general what they think, like, or believe. There are a lot of surveys to find out how people will vote in an election. But I could also survey you to find out in general how many of you like popcorn. Let's try it. How many of you like popcorn? Raise your hands. Okay, in general my survey of you shows that eighteen out of twenty-one students in this class like popcorn."

5. **asked students to give their own examples.** "Tell about something you could survey to get a general overview. Try to use *survey* when you tell about it. You could start by saying something like, 'I could survey . . .'"

6. **asked students to say the word again.** "What's the word we've been talking about?"

Then, Carl took his vocabulary lesson one step further. He

7. **asked students to keep track of the new word.** "Keisha, during work time today, would you please write the word *survey* on the vocabulary chart and give it a definition so we can remember this word. What would be a good definition for it?"

Carl and the students are keeping track of new vocabulary words by posting them on a vocabulary chart. Word collections are a way for awareness of and interest in words to be aroused.

The next day Carl used the same book, *All About Frogs*, in a shared reading format to foster word-learning strategies to help students learn new vocabulary on their own.

Second Lesson: Teaching Word-Learning Strategies

One reason that wide reading is an effective way to increase students' vocabularies may be because it is a quick way for students to experience many new words on their own. Carl teaches his students to use context clues for learning words on their own. He shows them how to read for definitions that are embedded right in the text. He also shows them a two-step process for figuring out the meaning of words when the definition is not explicit: 1) Use what you already know about the subject and 2) substitute other words that make sense for the word.

In this lesson, Carl is teaching his students how to use the context to figure out the word *accommodate* in this passage from *All About Frogs*: "A frog's head is wide to accommodate a huge mouth. Frogs swallow food whole." Carl usually tries to use familiar material, because it is easier to learn a new strategy when you are very familiar with the content already. Not only had his students heard him read *All About Frogs*, but they were also very familiar with the wide, smiling faces of frogs from their science unit and a field trip to a marsh where they had seen and handled frogs. In addition, Carl knew the students had a concept for how smaller objects could fit within a larger object. For example, bigger clothes *accommodate* or fit bigger people; a bigger room can *accommodate* or hold more people.

In the transcript below Carl explains how to use a two-step process to infer the meaning of new words when the definition is implicit. Then, he collaborates with and guides his students as they attempt to use the two steps on another word. These two steps will be familiar to you from Duke and Pearson's (2002) framework for explicit teaching of comprehension processes discussed in chapters 2 and 7. Their framework for explicit teaching can be used anytime you need to teach students how to use strategies or thinking processes. The model is also appropriate for teaching lower-level processes, such as sight-word learning, which you will see in Chapter 9.

Carl: You are getting very good at looking for definitions of words that the author puts right into the text. Today, I'm going to show you how to use other information when the author does not give you the definition right in the text. [*Carl shows the sentences from the text on the overhead and reads them out loud.*] If you did not know the word *accommodate*, how would you figure out what it meant? Here's how I do it.

Carl: I already know that a frog's head has to be very wide because a frog has a very big mouth—frogs eat their food whole in one big gulp. I ask myself, "If I left out the word *accommodate*, what other words would make sense in the sentence?" Let's see, *hold* would make sense: A frog's head is wide to hold a huge mouth. *To make room for* would also make sense: A frog's head is wide to make room for a huge mouth. Therefore, I know that *accommodate* must mean "hold" or "make room for."

> Explicit modeling: use what you know.

> Explicit modeling: thinking about other words that make sense in the sentence.

Carl: To figure out the meaning of the word *accommodate*, I first used what I knew already about frogs, and second, I thought of what other words would make sense in the context.

Explicit modeling: summarizing the two-step processes.

In the second portion of the lesson, Carl asks the students to try the strategy to learn the Tier Two word *thrusts*. Again, he already knew they had a concept for "push out quickly with force," and they knew how frogs used their tongues.

Carl: Try using 1) what you already know about frogs and 2) other words that make sense in the sentence to come up with a definition for the word *thrusts* in the next sentence. [*Carl displays this sentence on the overhead and reads it out loud.*] "A frog's most powerful muscles are its leg muscles and the muscle that rapidly thrusts its tongue out to snap up insects." First what do you already know about how a frog uses his tongue?

Collaborative/guided practice.

Matthew: A frog unrolls its long tongue and sucks up insects.

Carl: Good, you've used your prior knowledge about frogs. Who could suggest other words you could use instead of *thrusts* in the sentence?

Sierra: *Pushes*—the muscle that rapidly pushes its tongue out.

Carl: That's a good substitution. *Pushes* and *thrusts* mean the same in this sentence. Can anyone suggest another word for *thrusts*?

Tony: How about *spear*?

Carl: Let's see how it would sound in the sentence: The muscle that rapidly *spears* its tongue out to snap out insects. Does that mean exactly the same thing as *thrusts* or *pushes*? It doesn't seem to quite capture the meaning. You can thrust a spear, but to spear something wouldn't you have to have a sharp point? The frog snaps up its prey with a sticky tongue, like flypaper. The tongue is not really sharp like a spear. *Thrusts* means that you push out quickly with force.

Carl knows that second graders will need much guided practice with this strategy for inferring the meaning of words in a sentence. He will continue to focus on it in read-alouds and shared and guided reading lessons before expecting students to use the strategy independently. Again, this is an example of how a research framework for explicit teaching can be implemented flexibly, and over time, to achieve the desired results—students using the processes independently.

◆ ◆ ◆ Final Thoughts ◆ ◆ ◆

In this chapter you saw how vocabulary development in early primary contexts is a matter of fostering word consciousness through rich conversations as well as providing explicit instruction. Often, vocabulary development is readily integrated with comprehension and fluency instruction or in content area studies. Judith Irwin, author of *Teaching Reading Comprehension Processes* (1991), says that teaching methods that require students to hear and use words in meaningful ways, orally and in writing, for authentic purposes are more likely to result in robust vocabulary learning. Therefore, read-aloud, shared reading, interactive writing, and content area studies are instructional contexts that are particularly well suited to teaching vocabulary to young readers and writers. In the next chapter you will see how those same methods are used to foster fluency as well.

CHAPTER 9

Fluency

Effective Teaching to Foster Reading Fluency

R ead it again!" shouted the preschoolers as Melissa Anderson finished reading the story *I Know an Old Lady Who Swallowed a Fly* by Simms Taback (Viking, 1997). Melissa explained to the children that this story is also a song. They sang the song together and then returned to the book. Melissa and the children sang the words as Melissa ran her finger under the words. The children were learning to use appropriate phrasing. "I want the old lady to swallow me," said Ben as the story concluded. Melissa and the children continued to sing the story, having the old lady swallow the preschoolers. As these preschoolers listen to and participate in stories and songs, they are building a foundation for fluent reading.

Overview of the Chapter

The purpose of this chapter is twofold: to show how to foster reading fluency using research-based methods and to demonstrate how instruction changes as children develop. Consistently focusing on teaching for fluency in ways that are appropriate for children's development and grade levels, should help all children achieve rate norms (see Chapter 4) for oral and silent reading by the end of second grade. For example, singing songs and read-alouds in preschool lay the foundation for fluent oral reading during shared reading and guided reading lessons in first and second grades and for real-world oral reading occasions: performing scripts, giving speeches, making public announcements, offering toasts, reporting news, telling jokes, or shouting cheers (Rasinski, 2003, p. 22). First, we briefly review the research on fluency and then give examples of teaching for fluency in preschool through second-grade classrooms.

Review of the Research on Fluency

As discussed in Chapter 4, there are four components of fluent reading:

- **Accuracy:** correct pronunciation of words relative to the context (e.g., *read* pronounced as *reed* or *red*).

- **Expression:** reading in larger phrase chunks and conveying mood or feeling through changing voice tone—pauses, emphases, and pitch variations.

- **Comprehension:** prior knowledge of the world and past experience used to interpret, infer, connect with, understand, and evaluate an author's intended meaning.

- **Appropriate rate:** speed at which words are correctly pronounced relative to the purposes of the reader.

Therefore, fluency instruction in the primary grades must foster students' precursor and early abilities in those four areas. Questions to keep in mind as you plan instruction are listed in the box on this page.

Expression (i.e., phrasing and voice) and comprehension are closely related and form one major area for fluency instruction. In the early years you help young readers build an "ear" for how expressive oral reading sounds, and you teach them to read with phrasing and voice so that they can interpret and infer emotion and expression in text read orally or silently.

Accuracy and rate also are related because they are measures of rapid, automatic word recognition and decoding. In the early grades you help young readers build a foundation of sight words and phonics skills to enable them to read quickly and accurately, both orally and silently. Therefore, for each grade level, preschool through grade two, we collapsed the four dimensions into two major areas for fluency instruction: 1) oral reading expression and 2) sight word recognition and decoding. We refer exclusively to instruction for oral reading fluency since oral reading is the norm in the primary school, and since research shows that fluent oral reading contributes to the ability to read silently with fluency and comprehension (Rasinski, 2003; Samuels, 2002).

> ### Designing Research-Based Instruction for Fluency
>
> **Key questions for teachers:**
>
> - Am I helping students build a sight word vocabulary by teaching sight words, using a word wall, and providing lots of opportunities for students to reread familiar texts?
>
> - Am I helping students learn how to read orally with phrasing and expression through explicit teaching and activities that require students to reread familiar text for an audience (e.g., shared reading, Readers Theater)?
>
> - Am I helping students learn how to use comprehension strategies so that they can infer expression?
>
> - Am I helping students build their reading rate by providing lots of opportunities for them to reread familiar text and by explicitly explaining the need to read fluently to maintain meaning?

Teaching to Foster Fluency

Diane Lapp, James Flood, and Nancy Roser (2000) note:

> **Young children have enormous capacity for language learning.
> They delight in the sounds and meanings of new words, rolling
> the names of dinosaurs off their tongues, for example. But oral
> language development is more than facility with labels: it is com-
> ing to understand the need for precision, purpose, and audience
> in using language. (p. 187)**

That same understanding of the need for "precision" (accuracy and rate),
"purpose" (comprehension and rate), and "audience" (expression) is critical
in fluent reading. Again, oral language provides the foundation for understanding and using written language effectively. In the following sections,
you'll visit several classrooms to see how effective teaching can foster fluency
development.

Teaching for Fluency in PRESCHOOL

Exposure, Play, and Sensitive Instruction

Through singing songs and by being read to, preschoolers learn how oral
and written language sound, laying the foundation for oral reading expression. Here is how one preschool teacher, Angela Payne, whom you met in
Chapter 8, prepares her preschoolers for later oral reading fluency.

Laying a Foundation for Oral Reading Expression

It is now 8 A.M. Angela claps her hands and begins to sing:

> **Come, come, come to the circle,**
> **Come, come, come to the circle,**
> **Come, come, come to the circle,**
> **It's time to hear a story.**

The children join in the song as they put away the center materials and
join Angela on the rug.

Preschool children often repeat the phrases learned through songs and
stories during play. While playing with plush characters from Winnie the
Pooh, Sarah remarked, "Oh, bother!" when one of the characters fell over.
On another occasion, Kim reacted to her family's purchase of new furniture
by trying it out, just like Goldilocks. "This couch is too hard. This chair is
too soft, but this footstool is just right!" Thoughtful teachers have led these

children to an understanding that stories and songs need to be phrased and fluent. These children will carry this understanding into the next steps toward becoming readers themselves.

Laying a Foundation for Sight Word Recognition and Decoding

Preschoolers build a precursor skill for rapid, accurate sight word recognition by beginning to learn how to recognize and distinguish between letters. However, as Marilyn Adams (1990) shows in her review of the research, while the ability to name letters is a superlative predictor of reading achievement even through the seventh grade, it is not the naming of letters that is the salient factor. It is familiarity with how letters look. Letter recognition is the critical first step in word recognition. Unless young readers are wholly familiar with the identities of individual letters, they are not able to attend to the predictable patterns of letters that consistently form words and syllables.

Letter recognition is the ability to recognize and distinguish among the unique features (e.g., sticks, balls, or curves) of individual letters. For example, *b* and *d* and *p* and *q* share similar features, sticks and balls, but are identified by the way the sticks and balls are positioned—up or down, right side or left side. In effect, lowercase *b* and *d* or *p* and *q* form mirror images of each other. As another example, lowercase *u* and *n* share the distinguishing feature of a curve, but *u* is simply an upside-down curve while *n* is a right-side-up curve. Until a young child meets letters, nowhere else in life has position in space been such an important variable. A favorite doll or truck is still the same toy whether or not it is right side up or upside down. Chairs are still the same chairs whether or not they are on the right side or the left side of the table.

To make matters worse, letters are abstract objects that mean very little on their own, compared with emotionally meaningful objects, like a toy or a dog. In fact, letters may have little relevance to a young child's life—until she needs to learn how to read and write in school.

Furthermore, letters are usually flat, two-dimensional designs on paper, unlike most three-dimensional objects first encountered by young children. Therefore, letters require more-effortful perception. Marie Clay (1991) summarized the research of psychologists who have studied early child development. She reported that three- to seven-year-olds cannot visually isolate elements of a complex form, such as print, without appropriate training:

> **Research has shown that the three-year-old explores objects and forms manually by touching, manipulating, tracing with fingers and turning things over. The four- and five-year-old uses both**

> touch and visual exploration together to investigate shapes, supporting one with the other. By six years, many children can systematically explore forms and objects with their eyes alone. Such visual exploration involves a type of motor skill. (p. 285)

Learning to perceive printed letters requires both exposure and sensitive, age-appropriate instruction.

Exposure to letters in various sizes, textures, and hands-on forms—magnetic letters, felt letters, or sandpaper letters, for example—helps young children develop letter perception and builds a foundation for later word recognition and decoding. Learning the names of these shapes is less important in the preschool years than learning to look at and distinguish between the various features that make up letters.

Young children need to become flexible with letter recognition by having many opportunities to explore letters in various fonts and settings. Many parents place plastic magnetic letters on their refrigerator for their young children to manipulate. These same children see letters in newspapers and in environmental print. Children are particularly apt to notice the letters in the names of their favorite stores and restaurants. For several months Jacob called Toys R Us the *R* store. The prominent (although backward) *R* was easy for him to see and identify. When entering a restaurant with her parents, Katy asked her mother why the sign on the door said "no cookies." Katy had noticed the "No Checks" sign and used her knowledge of the sight word *no* and of the letter *C* to conclude that this restaurant did not have cookies. These are examples of children who are using what they know about letters, albeit not yet correctly, to interpret print in their environment.

"Sensitive instruction" includes making letters and words meaningful to children. Helping young children to recognize and write their own names is a first step. Many teachers use a name chart to assist with teaching the letters. These simple charts are valuable teaching tools. To construct a name chart, teachers simply write each child's name as it appears alphabetically on a piece of large chart paper. The chart is put in a prominent place near the group reading and writing area. (See Figure 9.1.)

Figure 9.1

Miss Angela

Abby	Ignacio
Adam	Jonathan
Alex	José
Briana	Kim
Charlie	Luke
Charlotte	Maria
Devone	Nat
Grace	Sarah

As these preschoolers learn about the letter *A*, they are able to refer to the capital *A* in Abby's name and the lowercase *a*'s present in the names of many of the children in this class. Kindergarten and first-grade teachers make extensive use of name charts to teach both reading and writing. What better way to learn to read and write the /ch/ sound than by using the name of your friend Charlie! Being able to recognize letters quickly will help these children become fluent readers. Recognizing letters is the first step in rapid, automatic word recognition.

Teaching for Fluency in KINDERGARTEN

A Focus on Shared Reading

Exposure, play, and sensitive teaching remain hallmarks of kindergarten learning as well. In addition, kindergartners need to continue building their "ears" for written language through lots of read-alouds and their "eyes" for looking at letters through continued exposure to letters in various shapes, sizes, and textures. However, kindergartners are typically ready for another level of fluency instruction: explicit talk about reading with expression and a focus on building a corpus of known letters, sounds, and sight words through shared reading.

Shared reading is an instructional method well suited to fostering reading fluency. It makes the reading process visible, explicitly teaching students how to navigate text. Reading strategies are modeled and practiced, and fluent reading is fostered through repeated readings of a favorite, familiar text.

During shared reading, the teacher and children sit close together and read together from a shared text. In kindergarten classrooms, the text is usually an enlarged text, called a "big book." Posters of poems, pieces of interactive writing, or overhead projections are also used.

In her book about shared reading, *Read It Again!* Brenda Parkes (2000) writes:

> **The first purpose of shared reading is to provide children with an enjoyable reading experience, to introduce them to a variety of authors and illustrators and the way these communicators craft meaning, and to entice them to want to be readers themselves. The second, equally important purpose is to teach children systematically and explicitly how to be readers and writers themselves. It is this second purpose that distinguishes shared reading from read-aloud. (pp. 1–2)**

Fostering a Foundation for Oral Reading Expression

Here's how kindergarten teacher Donna Cain used *Mrs. Wishy-Washy* by Joy Cowley (Philomel, 1990), a story about a harried farm wife who just cannot keep the naughty farm animals out of the mud, to foster expression and sight word learning. She also used it to foster comprehending processes, such as predicting and summarizing. She could have used it for a vocabulary lesson as well. Shared reading is an excellent teaching method to foster all the meaning-making systems for reading.

Figure 9.2

A Model for Explicit Instruction

1. Explicit description of the strategy and when and how it should be used (as in a mini-lesson: the most teacher help).

2. Teacher and/or student modeling of the strategy in action (as in interactive read-aloud or shared reading).

3. Collaborative use of the strategy in action (as in shared reading or interactive read-aloud).

4. Guided practice using the strategy with gradual release of responsibility (as in guided reading).

5. Independent use of the strategy (as in independent literature conversations or independent reading: the least teacher help).

Duke & Pearson, 2002, pp. 208–210.

After reading *Mrs. Wishy-Washy* several times so children could enjoy and appreciate the story (especially the naughty animals and the distraught Mrs. Wishy-Washy!), Donna brought the children's attention to a word in bold in the text. She used the boldface word to begin teaching the kindergartners how a reader changes voice pitch to convey expression and meaning. The picture on page 9 shows a frustrated Mrs. Wishy-Washy with her hand on her forehead and her mouth held open in a scream. The text reads:

"Just look at you!" she screamed.

As you read Donna's lesson, notice how she uses the research-proven instructional sequence (see Figure 9.2) outlined by Duke and Pearson (2002).

Donna: I want you to notice something on this page. See how the author has made this word [*pointing to* look] extra large and dark? Now notice how I read that. [*Donna points and reads, emphasizing the word* look.] Why do you suppose the word *look* is so large and dark?

Jeremy: Because Mrs. Wishy-Washy is yelling it!

Donna: Yes, she is screaming. And why is she screaming?

Danielle: 'Cause the animals are all muddy, and she don't like it.

New Essentials for Teaching Reading in PreK–2

Donna: If I read this page like this [*Donna reads in a dull monotone*], it would not sound like Mrs. Wishy-Washy was upset or screaming. I've got to read this so that it really sounds like Mrs. Wishy-Washy is upset. [*Donna reads again with expression.*]

This is called "reading with expression." Good readers try to imagine how the character is feeling, and then they try to read as though the character were really speaking.

You try reading this just like an upset Mrs. Wishy-Washy with me while I point to the words. Remember to really emphasize that word *look*.

> Modeling the strategy.

> Explicit description of the strategy.

> Collaborative use of the strategy.

[*Everyone chimes in enthusiastically.*]

Donna: Now, who would like to try reading it alone as I point to the words?

Using other shared reading lessons throughout the year, Donna will continue to teach the children how to use the nuances of voice tone, pitch, and stress to read with expression. She will also encourage the children to try reading their familiar books to a buddy using expression.

Fostering a Foundation for Sight Word Recognition and Decoding

During the same shared reading lesson, Donna also taught the children a new sight word. She could have chosen any number of words because several high-frequency words are in the book: *in, it, the,* and even *look*. However, she chose to focus on the word *and*. It was a word that the children would find useful in both reading and writing. Most of the sight words taught in kindergarten should be the most frequently used words in writing and reading. (See Figure 4.2: The 107 Most Frequently Used Words in Written English in Chapter 4.) Donna used the same instructional sequence that you will now recognize as an adaptation of Duke and Pearson's (2002) explicit teaching model: 1) explicit teaching, 2) collaborative/guided practice, 3) individual or independent practice.

[handwritten: ✶ most frequently used words]

Donna: There is a word in this book, *and* [*points to word*], that you often need to read and write. Listen as I read this page and notice the word *and*.

> *"Oh, lovely mud,"*
> *said the cow,*
> *and she jumped in it.* (pp. 2–3)

Sandip, can you help me mark it with the sticky tape—let's use green tape today.

[Sandip uses the colored tape to cover and.*]*

Donna: Now, let's look closely at it so you can learn how to read and write it. It has three letters: *a-n-d*. Make it in the air with me. [*Donna turns so the children can see the letters oriented correctly as she and they make the word* and *in the air, giving directions for each letter.*]

A—start at the top, go around and down. N—start at the top, go down, go up, and make a hump. D—make the circle first—around, up, and down for the stick. Let's make it again. [*Donna gives directions for making the letters again as they all trace them in the air.*]

Donna: Now, turn to a partner and use his or her back to trace the word *and* with your finger—be gentle.

Donna: The word *and* is used on several pages. Listen as I read these two pages. See if you can hear and see the word *and*.

> *"Oh, lovely mud,"*
> *said the pig,*
> *and he rolled in it.* (pp. 4–5)

Andy, can you come up and find *and* on this page and cover it with the highlighting tape?

The lesson went on like this until all the *and*s were found and covered with the transparent green tape. Then the whole story was read together again, with Donna stopping and letting the children read *and* each time by themselves. Donna uses a similar procedure to teach letters and sounds during shared reading.

Shared reading is an ideal venue for fostering fluent reading. Repeated readings (Rasinski, 2003; Samuels, 2002) are built in naturally, so children get lots of practice reading fluently with support. After such a supported context for reading, most young children transition easily to guided reading and then to independent reading of a new book. While many children transition to guided reading during the kindergarten year, guided reading is the heart of the instructional program in first and second grades.

Teaching for Fluency in FIRST GRADE

A Focus on Guided Reading

First-grade instruction to foster reading fluency still includes read-alouds and shared reading. However, first graders usually begin the year with a small corpus of known sight words, and they know how to read left to right,

New Essentials for Teaching Reading in PreK–2

matching speech to print on repetitive texts (e.g., *Here is a dog. Here is a cat.*) They are ready for explicit instruction to foster fluency through guided reading lessons.

Building the Foundation for Oral Reading Expression

In the following guided reading lesson, Kim Mendoza used a level F (9) text, *Sally's Friends* by Beverley Randell (1994) from Rigby's PM Collection. Kim was working with "early readers" who were just learning to read in phrases. Timothy Rasinski's research indicates that helping students to read in phrases will improve their reading fluency and overall reading achievement (1990, 1995, 2003).

After Kim introduced the book, the group read it for the first time to themselves with support from Kim as needed. Following the reading they discussed the important idea in the book about how to be a friend. Then, Kim used the book to teach the children how to read in phrases. This is not the first time they have heard about reading in phrases. However, she noticed that as they read to themselves, they were still not reading in phrases.

Kim: You have been working on reading in phrases. Good readers read in phrases because it helps them read faster, sound better when reading aloud, and understand the story better.

Turn to page 3 in your books. Listen as I read this page word by word. [*Kim reads word by word.*]

> *Sally/ went/ to/ play/ with/ Emma.*
> *"Can/ I/ climb/ up?"/ she/ said.*
> *"No,/ you/ can't,"/ said/ Emma.*
> *"Go/ away,/ Sally."*

See how choppy that sounds and not very interesting? Now listen to me read in phrases; see if you can tell where the phrases are. [*Kim reads with smooth, phrased expression.*] What did you think of that?

Maria: It sounds like talking.

Kim: That's how it is supposed to sound. Notice that this page is a conversation between Emma and Sally. How can you tell there is conversation?

Tyrell: It's got lots of talking marks?

Kim: Yes—those are called quotation marks. Everyone put your fingers around the first group of words in quotation marks. [*Everyone points to the words* "Can I climb up?"] This is Sally talking. This group of words goes together in a phrase. Try reading it with me all together in one go.

[Children read with Kim.]

> **Kim:** See how fast you read when you use just your eyes and say words in a phrase all together. *She said* is also read as a phrase. Try it with me.

[Children read she said.]

> **Kim:** I like how you read those two words together in a phrase. Now, let's read both phrases together. Use just your eyes—no fingers. Fingers don't look; eyes do.

[Children all read together: "Can I climb up?" she said.]

> **Kim:** Excellent phrasing! Now, use just your eyes to find the next phrase. When you find it, put your fingers around it to frame it.

[Children easily find "No, you can't."]

> **Kim:** I like how you all used your eyes to do the work. Take your fingers away and use just your eyes to read these two phrases together.

After Kim and the children finished looking at the individual phrases, they read the whole page together again, emphasizing the phrasing. Then, they turned to the next page and practiced recognizing and reading phrases here. The children did fine, as long as Kim was supporting them. They will need lots of review and practice to learn how to recognize and read with phrased, fluent reading. Several of the children in this group are still using their fingers to point to individual words, and this is slowing their reading and preventing them from reading in phrases.

Another step for this group and for many first graders is learning how to use punctuation as a guide to juncture—appropriate pausing in reading. This is key to reading with expression. Kim will use guided and shared reading lessons to introduce, reinforce, and provide practice for her first graders learning to use punctuation and phrasing to read smoothly with expression.

Marie Hayes, another first-grade teacher, introduced her students to a rubric to help them evaluate their own and one another's oral reading fluency. (See Figure 9.3.) Her students keep their laminated tagboard strip to use in guided reading groups and when buddy reading. Marie introduced her students to the rubric in shared reading format, carefully explaining and modeling how each category sounds. She says this has made a big difference in helping students take on phrased, fluent reading.

Of course, first graders still need to continue building a sight vocabulary of words that they can quickly recognize. They also need to learn more-complex decoding strategies. Rapid, automatic word recognition and quick

Figure 9.3

1	**2**	**3**	**4**
Word by word with long pauses.	Choppy. Mostly word by word.	Some longer phrased reading. Rereading for problem solving.	Fluent. Expressive. A few slowdowns for problem solving. Reading like a teacher.

decoding are also hallmarks of reading fluency. You can use shared and guided reading in first grade to teach for these components of fluency as well. There are many professional books available to help you with this (e.g., *Sound Systems* by Lyon & Moore, 2003). In the next section, on teaching for fluency in second grade, one of the sample lessons is a phonics lesson. The specific decoding skills you teach will vary depending on the children's developmental needs, but the lesson format could be adapted for first grade.

Teaching for Fluency in SECOND GRADE

A Focus on Practice, Practice, Practice!

Typically, second grade marks a transition to silent reading. The texts students can read are longer and more complex. Children have acquired a substantial number of words they can automatically recognize; they usually can decode longer and more-complex words if needed, and they can read more independently. But they still need to read more efficiently and quickly to be considered "fluent readers." This takes practice, practice, and more practice. While you still use read-alouds, shared reading, and guided reading, effective instruction to foster fluency will also include many opportunities for students to read aloud for a variety of purposes and audiences.

In addition, second graders are learning more about reading nonfiction texts. In kindergarten and first grade, you will read many nonfiction books aloud to the students; in second grade, typical students have more control over the reading process, and they can learn to use comprehending processes to read nonfiction independently. And they also must learn to apply what they have learned about reading fiction fluently to read a nonfiction text with smooth, phrased reading.

Extending the Foundation for Oral Reading Expression to Nonfiction Text

Again we visit Carl Porter's second-grade classroom, this time for a lesson to foster reading in phrases and using voice pitch and stress to read nonfiction text more fluently and expressively. After reading Jim Arnosky's book *All About Frogs* (Scholastic, 2002) to students in a science unit on amphibians, Carl makes overhead transparencies of several pages of the book to use as a shared reading lesson for the whole class. In the first lesson, Carl teaches his second graders about changes in voice pitch and stress to convey expression; in the second lesson, he reinforces the use of phrasing in fluent reading. The same sequence for explicit instruction outlined by Duke and Pearson (see Figure 9.2) is labeled so you can clearly see how it unfolds.

First Lesson: Use of Voice to Convey Expression

Carl: One of the things you have been working on in your reading is expression. Today, I'd like you to think about how you could read a nonfiction passage with expression. Let's look at this page about North American tree frogs from *All About Frogs*. [*Carl uses colored highlighting tape to mark two sentences on the overhead.*]

> *Because of their small size and plant-climbing lifestyle, tree frogs are much harder to spot than other frogs. Some, like the spring peeper tree frogs, are so small that you cannot find them even when you follow the sound of their call!*

Carl: Remember, we talked about how punctuation can give you some hint about expression. Commas tell us to pause briefly, and your voice goes down. But punctuation does not tell you everything. You can choose to emphasize certain words to make it more interesting for the listeners.

Listen and follow along with your eyes as I read these two sentences. Notice how my voice sounds at the commas, and notice how I emphasize certain words to make my voice more interesting to listen to. [*Carl reads the sentences, emphasizing pauses and voice pitch. He marks the overhead with a little arrow using an overhead marker to show how voice goes up and down, and underlines words that are emphasized.*]

Now, you all try reading these sentences with me, and try to make your voice pause and go up or down in the places I've marked, and try to emphasize the words I did to make your voices sound interesting.

[Students read sentences several times with Carl leading.]

Explicit description of the strategy.

Modeling the strategy.

Collaborative use of the strategy.

Carl: Would someone like to try reading this alone? We'll all listen and watch the text with our eyes.

Guided/independent practice using the strategy.

[Several students try reading the sentences alone. Carl supports the reading when needed.]

Carl: Okay, let's all read this together again.

Carl uses the same overhead during this lesson to review phrasing in fluent reading. Students have been learning about phrasing since first grade, but now they learn to apply that skill to a nonfiction text.

Second Lesson: Teaching for Phrasing

Carl: You've learned about reading in phrases so you're reading faster and more smoothly in stories or fiction text. Now you have to think about how to read in phrases in nonfiction text to also read more quickly and smoothly. Again, sometimes, there are no punctuation marks in a sentence to guide you. And then, you have to remember to read in larger chunks, or phrases, to make the reading sound smooth. Let's try that with the next sentence [*Carl marks the whole sentence with highlighting tape*]:

> *Tree frogs can quickly change their colors to blend with their surroundings.*

Explicit description of the strategy.

Carl: I would read this sentence in three chunks or groups. Listen to how I read it and follow with your eyes. See if you can tell the three chunks. "Tree frogs/ can quickly change their colors/ to blend with their surroundings." Talk to the person next to you about where you think I grouped the words.

Modeling the strategy.

[Students talk in pairs.]

Carl: Okay, here's where I grouped the words. [*Reads sentence again and uses overhead marker to indicate breaks between word groups.*] How many people heard these groups when I read? Let's all read this together, and group the words like I did.

More modeling the strategy.

Collaborative use of the strategy.

There are many directions in which you might go to provide students with more guided and independent practice, depending on their ability. For example, you might want to let students try reading the next sentence with a buddy to see where they would group the words. Or you might just end the lesson and pick up instruction for expression during guided reading. Next, you will see how Carl uses a guided reading lesson to teach phonics.

Extending the Foundation for Sight Word Recognition and Decoding

In keeping with his focus on nonfiction text, Carl uses nonfiction texts for his second-grade guided reading groups as well. He tries to find at least one text suitable for each group that carries over the content area theme the class is working on. For the theme on amphibians, Carl chose the book *Frog* by Angela Royston (Lodestar Books, 1991), from the Dorling Kindersley series See How They Grow to use with Nathan, Miranda, and Spencer. They are reading below second-grade expectations at Level H (13/14) after the first quarter, ten weeks, of instruction. You met this group having the first part of their guided reading lesson on recognizing and using nonfiction text structures to help comprehension in Chapter 7. Carl finishes that lesson by focusing on decoding longer words. This is another example of how teaching for comprehension, vocabulary, and fluency are often part of the same lesson context.

After students finish reading and talking about one new thing they learned about frogs, Carl used words in the book *Frog* to help them learn more about analyzing longer words. Carl knew from the phonics test he gave for the first-quarter grade report that Nathan, Miranda, and Spencer know most common short and long vowel patterns in many common one-syllable words, but they need to begin working on analyzing multisyllabic words. This is typical for transitional readers. (See Lyon & Moore, 2003, for a more thorough description of phonics instruction for typical transitional readers.) Carl begins by reviewing a concept he has worked on recently, compound words, and then moves into an instructional sequence focused on helping the students learn how to analyze longer, multisyllabic words. You can probably identify that typical instructional sequence yourself.

Carl: Last week we talked about compound words. [*Carl briefly reviews the concept of compound words and students practice separating several words on the board.*]

> **Periodic review of concepts taught.**

There is a compound word on page nine. When you find it, put your finger on it and look at me. [*Students successfully find* underwater.]

[*Then, Carl turns to helping students identify common word parts in another word,* surrounded.]

Carl: Now turn back to page seven. I'm going to show you how to find parts you know in other longer words when they are not compound words. Miranda, please read that part at the top of the page.

Miranda: [*Reads correctly.*] "Each black egg is surrounded by clear jelly, and they all stick together."

[*Carl demonstrates how to take apart the word* surrounded *by taking off the ending, -ed, and the prefix, sur-. They quickly recognize the familiar word* round.]

Carl: When you see a long word you don't know, try taking off the ending and then look for word parts you know. You know that the first part, *sur-*, looks like *fur*. That helps you know how to pronounce it. You also know some other words that begin with *sur-*, like *surprise*. Then you saw the word you knew, *round*. Once you take the word apart and recognize the pieces, then you put it back together again: *sur/round/ed*. Let's try that with some other words. [*They take apart* surface *and* hatched.]

These were all good words to practice decoding because they were familiar to the students from the context. When students are just learning a new decoding principle, try to teach it using words the students have read in context; if they have the meaning of the word, they can use their cognitive resources to focus on just the new decoding principle. Branch out to help students apply decoding principles on totally unknown words when they can use the new principle effectively.

Opportunity for Extended-Reading Practice

One of the usual hallmark changes in development at the second-grade level is students' ability to read and write more independently. By the middle of the year, most of Carl's second graders are reading two books at once, one for guided reading and one for their literature conversation group. They keep the books in their own desks, and Carl does not organize a separate, whole-group time for independent rereading of familiar text. However, if students are reading significantly below grade level, Carl provides center-type activities or book boxes for these students to use independently. The key to making all this activity run smoothly is to have both the teacher and students know what they will be doing during the independent work time. Carl usually makes a chart each day that outlines what everyone will be doing, including himself. In Figure 9.4, you can see an example of one day's independent work. Free reading and continuing to work on a project or a writing draft are always options during independent work time if students finish the assigned work. In general, Carl groups students with the same needs for guided reading or literature conversations.

Carl usually spends the first six weeks of school establishing routines and slowly easing students into extended reading and writing as they transition out of learning centers. It often takes until the middle of the year for second

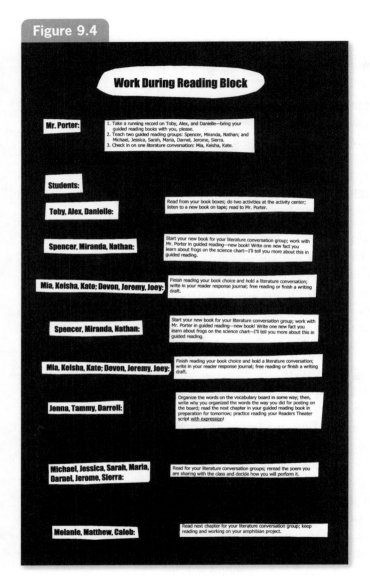

Figure 9.4

Work During Reading Block

Mr. Porter:
1. Take a running record on Toby, Alex, and Danielle—bring your guided reading books with you, please.
2. Teach two guided reading groups: Spencer, Miranda, Nathan; and Michael, Jessica, Sarah, Maria, Darnel, Jerome, Sierra.
3. Check in on one literature conversation: Mia, Keisha, Kate.

Students:

Toby, Alex, Danielle: Read from your book boxes; do two activities at the activity center; listen to a new book on tape; read to Mr. Porter.

Spencer, Miranda, Nathan: Start your new book for your literature conversation group; work with Mr. Porter in guided reading—new book! Write one new fact you learn about frogs on the science chart—I'll tell you more about this in guided reading.

Mia, Keisha, Kate; Devon, Jeremy, Joey: Finish reading your book choice and hold a literature conversation; write in your reader response journal; free reading or finish a writing draft.

Spencer, Miranda, Nathan: Start your new book for your literature conversation group; work with Mr. Porter in guided reading—new book! Write one new fact you learn about frogs on the science chart—I'll tell you more about this in guided reading.

Mia, Keisha, Kate; Devon, Jeremy, Joey: Finish reading your book choice and hold a literature conversation; write in your reader response journal; free reading or finish a writing draft.

Jenna, Tammy, Darrell: Organize the words on the vocabulary board in some way; then, write why you organized the words the way you did for posting on the board; read the next chapter in your guided reading book in preparation for tomorrow; practice reading your Readers Theater script with expression!

Michael, Jessica, Sarah, Maria, Darnel, Jerome, Sierra: Read for your literature conversation groups; reread the poem you are sharing with the class and decide how you will perform it.

Melanie, Matthew, Caleb: Read next chapter for your literature conversation group; keep reading and working on your amphibian project.

graders to learn how to work fairly independently during extended reading and writing time.

Opportunities for extended reading practice are critical in second grade. Research clearly shows that extended reading time fosters fluency (Rasinski, 2003; Samuels, 2002). During independent work time, students in Carl's classroom may be reading independently in preparation for guided reading groups or literature conversations, practicing oral reading for a Readers Theater production, writing in response to reading, or reading and writing as part of project work. The second graders in Carl's classroom are constantly reading for a purpose: to find out information for inquiry projects, to prepare for guided reading or literature discussions, or in preparation for a reading performance, such as Readers Theater. *The Fluent Reader* by Timothy V. Rasinski (2003) includes many suggestions for ways to read orally for various purposes and audiences. The context for all the reading is authentic, and the materials students read are on their levels and of interest to them. They hardly know they are practicing, practicing, practicing!

♦ ♦ ♦ Final Thoughts ♦ ♦ ♦

In Chapter 4 we talked about conditions for effective learning in general and applied them to learning how to read fluently. Here are those conditions again (Samuels, 2002, p. 172):

1. **Motivation:** Students need lots of reading material that they find interesting and pleasurable to read.

2. **Instruction:** Students need explicit, specific instruction in how to read fluently with phrasing and appropriate expression. They also need instruction in decoding, word analysis skills, and word building.

3. **Extended practice:** Students need opportunities for extended practice of fluent reading in ways that are motivating and authentic. They need texts that are on easy and instructional levels to accomplish this.

Each of the classrooms we profiled in this chapter provided examples of how these conditions are met in developmentally appropriate ways:

- **Preschoolers** are exposed to fluent reading through songs, oral language play, read-alouds, and a focus on their names and the names of their friends.

- **Kindergartners** explore elements of fluent reading, including expression and sight word and letter learning, through shared reading lessons.

- **First graders** learn to read fluently through guided reading lessons that include explicit instruction in the elements of reading for expression as well as decoding skills.

- **Second graders** practice fluent reading through opportunities for extended independent work, explicit instruction on more-complex texts, and performances for a variety of purposes and audiences.

Ideally, your team of preschool to second-grade teachers can work together to establish a developmental sequence of instruction for teaching comprehending processes, vocabulary, and fluency. In Chapter 10 we present suggestions for professional development to help your team meet its goals for ensuring that all learners achieve success in reading by the time they enter third grade.

Professional Development

Facilitating School Conversations About Comprehension, Vocabulary, and Fluency Instruction

In the spring of 2003, we took a look at our reading scores and found that comprehension was an issue across the board. The assistant principal, Jeanna Tuelle, and I talked about how we could help teachers with their comprehension instruction and decided that a book study group was the way to go. We put out feelers and found that we had 20 K–4 teachers who were interested in participating in monthly meetings around a book we read in common. We were pleased, because this is about one third of our faculty.

Jeanna ordered the book we chose and it was ready for us in the fall when we returned to school. We asked teachers to read one or two chapters every month, and we met after school to talk about what we had read. Most of our sessions took pretty much the same form. We started the sessions by having teachers share what they had been doing in their classrooms, and then we split into small groups to talk about what we had read that month and how that might look in the classroom. Then we came back together to share the "Big Ideas."

It wasn't long before teachers were saying they wanted to adopt particular instructional practices related to teaching for comprehending strategies. Jeanna found some money for teachers to work for a couple of days in the summer of 2004. During that summer, we

♦ established a scope and sequence for teaching comprehending strategies in our school,

♦ found resources in the school that we already had and created a resource notebook for each teacher,

♦ developed at least two lessons to go with each comprehending strategy, and

♦ made a list of resources that we'd like to purchase in the future. We are now looking for grant money for books, etc.

Best of all, teachers agreed that they wanted to keep meeting. New professional books have been bought and passed out to teachers. Teachers who did not take part in the study group have been given materials and asked to incorporate comprehending strategies into their teaching. They are being encouraged to ask for help from Jeanna, me, or any other teachers as they try out teaching these new strategies. I just got a copy of the new report card, and the comprehending strategies are included on it.

One of the exciting things for me was that it really sent a message to teachers that we need to be teaching comprehension but that we will help you figure out how to do that! Teachers also felt free to try out new things.

The push to incorporate comprehending strategies into our curriculum came from the teachers but was supported fully by the administration. I think another key to making it work is that we aren't letting it go. We'll keep on meeting and talking this year and I am guessing in the future.

—Sharon Greaney, Literacy Specialist and Reading Recovery Teacher Leader, Old Town Elementary School, Old Town, Maine

This example demonstrates the power of informal reflective practice groups in a school setting. As Sharon said later, "It changed the talk in the teachers' room!"

Overview of the Chapter

Our goal in this chapter is to help you use this book in a reflective practice study group. The chapter will help you facilitate conversations in your school about the importance of talk in teaching and about using research-based practices in teaching for comprehension, vocabulary, and fluency. We describe the factors that create a school climate that supports reflective practice study groups and present information on the nuts and bolts of scheduling them. Finally, we provide our specific suggestions for exploring the four topic areas covered in this book: talk as a vehicle for teaching, comprehension, vocabulary, and fluency.

Creating a School Climate to Foster Reflective Practice Study Groups

Informal reflective-practice study groups work best when teachers come together voluntarily to explore a book on a topic that interests them. Creating a school climate that fosters voluntary reflective practice study groups is the first step. Sharon's story of how Old Town Elementary School implemented newer practices for teaching comprehension revealed some important elements that must be present for effective professional development and instructional change. It provides a model for us.

Participating Is Voluntary. While Sharon, the literacy specialist, and Jeanna, the assistant principal, identified comprehension as a priority based on school assessment data, they did not say that teachers *had* to attend the group. Nor did they say that the purpose of the group was to "improve comprehension scores." They presented comprehension as a topic for inquiry and invited the teachers to participate in an exploration. There wasn't even an explicit expectation that "you will improve your teaching" or that everybody had to participate.

Who Initiates the Reflective Practice Group Is Important. It needs to be someone who is perceived by the teachers as a person who "helps us" rather than someone who "evaluates us." The school literacy specialist is the ideal person to initiate and facilitate a reflective practice group. As a literacy specialist, Sharon was in a unique position to facilitate because her official role in the school hierarchy is to support literacy curriculum and instruction.

Support From the Administration Is Important. As assistant principal, Jeanna was able to supply the resources to buy books and support summer work. By participating in the reflective practice study group herself, she communicated implicitly that comprehension is an important area of instruction. And when teachers began generating materials and lessons for the resource notebook, she communicated her value for their professional decision making and work by seeing that the school curriculum and the report card system reflected their work.

Maintain Support for the Core Group of Teachers Who Initiated the Curriculum Changes. Sharon identified the key to implementing comprehension instruction work: "We aren't letting it go. We'll keep on meeting and talking this year and I am guessing in the future." And she is right. Continued, sustained study on a topic is crucial to ensuring instructional change. One sure way to kill teacher enthusiasm is to jump constantly from educational bandwagon to bandwagon. This saps teacher energy and prevents any curriculum change from being fully adopted.

Reach Out to the Rest of the Staff. With a core group of enthusiastic teachers supporting the implementation of teaching for comprehending strategies, Jeanna and Sharon approached the two thirds of the faculty who had not been part of the initial reflective practice group. They were invited to begin exploring comprehension instruction, but now they had a gentle but explicit nudge to do so—the report card included comprehending strategies. But this time lots of other people were ready to help. Sharon said, "They are being encouraged to ask for help from Jeanna, me, or any other teachers as they try out teaching these new strategies." Another key to instituting newer practices is that the school climate fostered risk taking and collaboration and support between teachers. At Old Town Elementary School teachers feel free to ask one another, Sharon, or even Jeanna to help them as they try new practices and struggle to make the transition from theory into practice.

Keys to Creating a School Climate That Fosters Reflective Practice Study Groups

- Voluntary participation.
- Facilitator who is viewed as a "helper" rather than "evaluator" of teachers.
- Explicit support of the administration by providing resources for books, materials, and summer or extended-day teacher work and by integrating work of the group into the formal practices of the school (e.g., curriculum resource notebooks, report cards).
- Support by the administration demonstrated by its participation in the reflective practice study group and its taking an authentic inquiry stance on the topic (i.e., the answers will emerge from the group, not from the administration).
- Support for continued, sustained study on the topic (rather than jumping from hot topic to hot topic).
- Explicit support for those not involved in the initial study of the topic; formal encouragement of teachers to seek the help of anyone on the staff as they try to implement new, research-based practices.
- A focus on fostering authentic understandings that emerge from the study group, rather than on improving test scores or meeting federal mandates.
- Trust that the teachers in the reflective practice study group will grow in their professional knowledge and that that knowledge will impact the curriculum (but avoid trying to predict or mandate what that impact might be).

Create a School Climate for Reflective Practice Study Groups. Jeanna, Sharon, and the teachers did not focus on "improving school test scores," even though low comprehension scores were the impetus for the exploration. Instead, they focused on improving their understanding of comprehension through authentic exploration of the issue. This is the only way to ensure real change in instructional practice. Top-down mandates for change occasioned by test scores or federal legislation, such as the No Child Left Behind Act, seldom affect the real culture of teaching.

To change, teachers must have time to explore theory *and* practice and feel that they are initiating the curriculum changes with the support of the administration, rather than because of the administration. It is key that at Old Town Elementary School, curriculum change was perceived to be the result of teacher initiative. Sharon stated, "The push to incorporate comprehending strategies into our curriculum came from the teachers but was supported fully by the administration." It takes a school climate in which teachers feel supported and valued for their work. Initiators and facilitators for reflective practice study groups must trust that a new direction for the school will emerge from the study and resist trying to predict or shape that direction themselves.

Nuts and Bolts of Organizing an Informal Reflective Practice Study Group

Creating a school climate that fosters reflective practice study groups is the first and probably the most complex step. Implementing reflective practice groups is relatively easy. Sharon and Jeanna found that meeting with teachers after school on a monthly basis for about an hour and a half, across the school year, provided a workable schedule. It is important to take a whole year to focus on the one book or topic for study in order to give teachers enough time to *really* reflect on and try out newer practices. Sharon and Jeanna first met with the teachers who wanted to participate during the first professional development days before school opened. In this meeting they scheduled the remaining after-school meetings on a day each month, October until May, when all could attend; they also settled on a time for the meetings—3:00 to 4:30 P.M.

With all the other school or district initiatives that typically take place after school, monthly meetings made reflective practice study groups seem doable. Monthly meetings give teachers adequate time to read, reflect, and even try out new things in their classrooms before meeting again. In addition, most teachers don't feel as though they are sacrificing too much of their own time if the group meets after school on a monthly basis.

Ideally, reflective practice study groups can also be scheduled on regular district professional development days to supplement or substitute for several after-school meetings. Even better is scheduling meetings during the regular school day. This clearly communicates to teachers that these groups are an important and valued vehicle for teacher development and curriculum change.

In addition, many schools provide teachers with professional development credits for participation in reflective practice study groups. Teachers can apply these credits toward subsequent teacher recertification or meet goals for professional development plans. The more that reflective practice study groups can be integrated into the formal structure of the institution, the more it communicates how much the system values the work teachers are doing in the group.

Finally, Sharon and Jeanna created a predictable, informal, and pressure-free format for the monthly 90-minute meetings. Here's the format they followed:

1. Teachers shared what they have been doing in their classrooms around comprehension in the past month.

2. Teachers met in small groups to discuss the reading for the month.

3. The whole group met to share the "Big Ideas" from their discussions.

With Sharon and Jeanna's monthly 90-minute meeting schedule providing the general framework for operating a yearlong reflective practice study group, in the remaining portion of this chapter we suggest how you might focus your time during those meetings to cover the four topics in this book: talk as a vehicle for teaching, comprehension, vocabulary, and fluency.

A Yearlong Agenda to Foster Teacher Reflective Practice Using *New Essentials for Teaching Reading in PreK–2*

We present two ways that you might approach reflective practice study groups with this book. First, we outline a series of nine monthly meetings in which you and your teachers study all four topics covered in the book over one school year. Second, we present a format in which different groups of teachers study, in depth, particular topics in the book and present their findings to the rest of the faculty. The latter format is particularly recommended as a follow-up to a yearlong study that focuses on how comprehension, vocabulary, and fluency are interrelated and interdependent processes that can be integrated during instruction.

Studying All Four Topics

Most schools in North America have nine and a half months in each academic year. Therefore, we suggest a schedule of eight monthly meetings for a reflective practice study group to discuss this book and a ninth meeting to discuss "where do we want to go next?" In creating a schedule, it is best to avoid the first few weeks of school, when teachers are getting their classrooms up and running, and to spare them a meeting at the very end of school when they are dealing with closing down the classroom and finalizing record keeping.

After an introductory overview meeting, you might devote one meeting to the topic of "talk as a vehicle for teaching," and then two consecutive meetings apiece for the three other topics. For the topics of comprehension, vocabulary, and fluency, the first of two meetings should focus on the research chapter in Part I, and the second meeting should follow up with the corresponding research-into-practice chapter in Part II. For each meeting we suggest "essential questions" to guide the reading and discussion.

At the end of the overview meeting, ask the group to read both chapters on "talk" (1 and 6) for the next meeting. The importance of talk in the classroom is a theme that runs throughout the book; therefore, it is the first topic you study. Then, throughout the remaining discussions, you bring teachers' attention to the interdependence and interconnections between talk and teaching for comprehending, vocabulary, and fluency processes. That's really the "biggest" of the "Big Ideas" in this book.

Agenda for Reflective Practice Study Group Meetings

The following schedule assumes that you have met with the teachers beforehand to settle on dates and times for the nine meetings. The agendas for each meeting that you subsequently send out to teachers might look like the ones on pages 151–155.

New Essentials for Teaching Reading in PreK–2

Introductory Meeting:
Overview of the Book and Introduction
to Our Year of Study

Date/Time:

Please read the **Introduction** *and* **Chapter 5** *in* New Essentials for Teaching Reading in PreK–2 *by Moore and Lyon (2005) in preparation for our first meeting.*

Essential questions to guide our study: What foundation for comprehension, vocabulary, and fluency do young children bring with them when they come to school? How do we build on that foundation? Why should we teach for comprehension, vocabulary, and fluency in preK–2? What is research-based instruction and how can we integrate it into our classrooms?

1. Introduction to and overview of the book *New Essentials for Teaching Reading in PreK–2* by Moore and Lyon (2005)

2. Review of the year's meeting schedule and schema for studying the book

3. Small-group discussions of the Introduction and Chapter 5

4. Sharing "Big Ideas" from the Introduction and Chapter 5 with the whole group

Meeting Two:
The Importance of Talk in Teaching and Learning

Date/Time:

*Read **chapters 1 and 6**.*

Essential questions to guide our study: How and why are classroom talk and comprehension, vocabulary, and fluency instruction interconnected and interdependent? Why is talk so important for teaching comprehending, vocabulary, and fluency processes? Why is talk so important in early primary classrooms? How do children "talk to learn"?

1. Sharing ideas from our classrooms (about the importance of talk for teaching)
2. Small-group discussions of "The Importance of Talk in Teaching and Learning" (chapters 1 and 6)
3. Sharing "Big Ideas" about talk with the large group and discussing implications for our curriculum and instruction

Meeting Three:
Comprehension Research

Date/Time:

*Read **Chapter 2**.*

Essential questions to guide our study: How is comprehension different from but related to comprehending? What are comprehending processes and how can you teach them?

1. Sharing ideas from our classrooms (comprehension and talk)
2. Small-group discussions of Chapter 2
3. Sharing "Big Ideas" about comprehension research with the large group and discussing implications for our curriculum

Meeting Four:
Comprehension Research Into Practice

Date/Time:

*Read **Chapter** 7.*

Essential questions to guide our study: What are the research-based practices for teaching comprehending processes? To what extent does teaching comprehending processes change over time, from preschool to second grade? What would work in my classroom?

1. Sharing ideas from our classrooms (around talk or comprehension instruction)
2. Small-group discussions of Chapter 7
3. Sharing "Big Ideas" about comprehension instruction with the large group and discussing implications for our curriculum

Meeting Five:
Vocabulary Research

Date/Time:

*Read **Chapter** 3.*

Essential questions to guide our study: What does it mean to know a word? How is vocabulary related to comprehending? What and how many words should you teach? What's the best way to foster vocabulary development with young readers?

1. Sharing ideas from our classrooms
2. Small-group discussions of Chapter 3
3. Sharing "Big Ideas" about vocabulary research with the large group and discussing implications for our curriculum

Meeting Six:
Vocabulary Research Into Practice

Date/Time:

*Read **Chapter 8**.*

Essential questions to guide our study: What are the research-based practices for fostering vocabulary development? How does vocabulary instruction change over time, from preschool to second grade? What would work in my classroom?

1. Sharing ideas from our classrooms (around vocabulary instruction specifically)
2. Small-group discussions of Chapter 8
3. Sharing "Big Ideas" on vocabulary instruction with the large group and discussing implications for our curriculum

Meeting Seven:
Fluency Research

Date/Time:

*Read **Chapter 4**.*

Essential questions to guide our study: How is fluency related to comprehending? What are the three components of fluent reading? How do you assess fluent reading?

1. Sharing ideas from our classroom (talk, comprehension, vocabulary, or fluency)
2. Small-group discussions of Chapter 4
3. Sharing "Big Ideas" about fluency research with the large group and discussing implications for our curriculum

Meeting Eight:
Fluency Research Into Practice

Date/Time:

Read **Chapter 9**.

Essential questions to guide our study: What are the research-based practices for fostering fluency? How does teaching for fluency change over time, from preschool to second grade? What would work in my classroom?

1. Sharing ideas from our classrooms (talk, comprehension, vocabulary, or fluency)

2. Small-group discussions of Chapter 9

3. Sharing "Big Ideas" about fluency instruction with the large group and discussing implications for our curriculum

Meeting Nine:
Where Do We Want to Go From Here?

(How about meeting in a restaurant over dinner?)

Date/Time:

Please be prepared to share what you feel you have learned this year from our study of the importance of talk for teaching and comprehension, vocabulary, and fluency research. What do you think the implications are for our curriculum and instruction?

The advantage to studying all four topics in this book across the year is that it raises teachers' awareness of all these critical components for fostering students' abilities to read fluently for understanding. Studying the topics together also makes it possible to see how to foster comprehension, vocabulary, and fluency as integrated processes during instruction in regularly planned literacy contexts.

However, there is also some value in studying each topic in this book in depth. Teachers then can explore other resources outside this book to create a broader understanding of the topic. This might be a particularly effective way to approach a second year of study with the same teachers.

A Format for Reflective Practice Groups That Study Each Topic In Depth

Once teachers understand how reflective practice groups work, they can be in charge of their own groups to study a book or books and report back independently on their findings. Following is an eight-month schedule that combines suggested foci for monthly independent book study group meetings as well as two large-group sessions during which groups report on their independent work. The books listed for independent study groups are only suggestions by way of example. You or your teacher study groups may decide to study other books on the topics.

A two-year, focused study of the topics should help teachers refine their understandings and more easily begin to translate research into practice in classroom curriculum and instruction. However, to make the transition from research to practice, another step is often necessary—classroom coaching. On pages 157–159, we've included a very brief overview of how you could combine these reflective practice study groups with a classroom coaching model.

Month One:
Getting Organized for Independent Study Groups

Date/Time:

Please think about the book choices below and come prepared to make a choice—or to recommend another book for the topic. The books are in my office for you to examine.

1. Present overview of the independent study group format.
2. Brief book talk on each book under consideration for independent study group reading.
3. Choose a book for independent group study.
4. Plan a meeting schedule with the other members of your group.

The Importance of Talk for Teaching
Suggested book for study: *Choice Words: How Our Language Affects Children's Learning* by Peter Johnston (Stenhouse, 2004).

Comprehending Processes
Suggested books for study: *Knee to Knee, Eye to Eye: Circling In on Comprehension* by Ardith Davis Cole (Heinemann, 2003) or *Comprehension: Strategic Instruction for K–3 Students* by Gretchen Owocki (Heinemann, 2003).

Vocabulary
Suggested book for study: *Bringing Words to Life: Robust Vocabulary Instruction* by Isabel Beck, Margaret McKeown, and Linda Kucan (Guilford Press, 2002).

Fluency
Suggested book for study: *The Fluent Reader: Oral Strategies for Building Word Recognition, Fluency, and Comprehension* by Timothy Rasinski (Scholastic, 2003).

Months Two, Three, and Four:
Meet in Study Groups

Essential questions for our study: How does the reading link back to *New Essentials for Teaching Reading in PreK–2* by Paula Moore and Anna Lyon? What else have we learned about this topic? What does it mean for our curriculum and instruction?

1. Discuss the readings you assigned for yourself.
2. Share ideas from your classrooms.
3. Decide on tentative findings to share with the large group in month five.

Please let me know if you need any help.

Month Five:
Meet in Large Group to Share Tentative Findings

Date/Time:

1. Share your reactions and responses to the book you are reading: How does the book you are reading link back to *New Essentials for Teaching Reading in PreK–2* by Paula Moore and Anna Lyon?
2. Share ideas from your classrooms.
3. Evaluate how the format for independent study group is working.

Months Six and Seven:
Meet in Study Groups

Essential questions for our study: How does the reading link back to *New Essentials for Teaching Reading in PreK–2* by Paula Moore and Anna Lyon? What else have we learned about this topic? What does it mean for our curriculum and instruction?

1. Discuss the readings and share ideas from your classrooms.
2. Decide what ideas from your classrooms you will share with the large group.
3. Finalize recommendations for curriculum and instruction.

Please let me know if you need any help.

Month Eight:
Meet in Large Group

Date/Time:

1. Small groups share ideas from their topic area that they have tried out in their classrooms.
2. Groups make recommendations for next steps for curriculum and instruction.
3. Evaluate the year's format for independent study groups and make recommendations for next year's study group—format and topics.

Classroom Coaching Model

While teachers are studying a topic in reflective practice groups, it is useful to begin offering support to help them move the research into practice. Instructional change is most likely to happen when teachers have someone who can visit their classrooms and give them specific feedback on a particular instructional method they are attempting to implement. Everyone in a study group can be a coach for others. In fact, peers are often more effective as coaches because they are not viewed as evaluators. And the peers who are studying the same topic area are ideal as coaches; they are struggling with the same research-into-practice issues, and they will learn as much about implementing newer practices as the person being coached. In a peer-coaching situation, the learning always goes both ways. In addition, when teachers open their doors to trusted peers, it improves the learning/teaching climate of the whole school and creates an atmosphere of increased openness to instructional change in general.

Once study groups are under way, you can suggest that members of a study group begin visiting one another's classrooms to give help and feedback. In our experience working with either pre- or in-service teachers in our university classes, peer coaching typically involves these three steps:

1. Pre-conference in which the one to be coached relays how he or she wants help from the coach

2. Classroom observation of teaching

3. Post-conference in which the coach gives feedback and help to the person observed, focusing specifically on the help requested

Usually, the pre- and post-conferencing happens before or after school. The pre-conference should be very quick, and the coach should take good notes. Then the coach and teacher plan a time when the coach can visit the classroom to see the teacher teach a lesson on the focus area. Typically, coaches meet to debrief with their colleague after school or at another time when both are free from classroom duties.

In the pre-conference the coach structures the talk around these two points:

1. Tell me about the lesson you want me to watch.

2. Tell me what feedback and help you would like me to give you.

Then, during the classroom observation of teaching, the coach focuses just on the area requested by the teacher.

In the follow-up conference, the coach keeps strictly to the feedback or help requested by the teacher. Once coaches and teachers develop a thoroughly trusting relationship, coaches may branch out into other areas they noticed in the lesson where they could provide feedback or help.

These are some of the solutions schools have found to make time for a peer coach to visit another teacher's classroom:

♦ Teachers make visits when their students are having instruction from another teacher such as music, art, or gym.

♦ Teachers ask the principal or literacy specialist to cover their classrooms for half an hour.

♦ The school hires a substitute teacher for one day who circulates from classroom to classroom to release teachers to make visits.

It is important not to rush into peer coaching if the concept is totally new to the school. Teachers should first be comfortable with reflective practice study groups and trust that their work in the groups is valued and used. Then, peer coaching should be offered only on a volunteer basis, so you do not compromise the climate of trust and inquiry established by the study groups.

♦ ♦ ♦ Final Thoughts ♦ ♦ ♦

Throughout this book we have emphasized that comprehension, vocabulary, and fluency are interdependent variables in reading for meaning. Comprehension is compromised if a student lacks the vocabulary to understand a text or is unable to read fluently to maintain meaning in memory across longer stretches of text. Conversely, fluent reading with expression is compromised if students cannot infer characters' intentions or understand the plot. Likewise, vocabulary development is undermined if students cannot read for comprehension in order to use context to learn new word meanings. In preschool to second-grade classrooms, teaching for comprehending, vocabulary, and fluency processes is integrated naturally in typical and often informal contexts for instruction.

Improving reading comprehension, vocabulary, and fluency are important goals for any school, regardless of school test scores or state and federal mandates for accountability. Instructional change happens when teachers are truly invested in the change and have had a hand in shaping it. When you combine reflective practice study groups with a classroom peer-coaching model, you have an extremely powerful model for improving curriculum and instruction.

Professional References Cited

Adams, M. J. (1990). *Beginning to read: Thinking and learning about print.* Cambridge, MA: MIT Press.

Allen, J. (1999). *Words, words, words: Teaching vocabulary in grades 4–12.* Portland, ME: Stenhouse.

Allington, R. (1977). If they don't read much, how they ever gonna get good? *Journal of Reading, 21,* 57–61.

Anderson, C. (2000). *How's it going?: A practical guide to conferring with student writers.* Portsmouth, NH: Heinemann.

Anderson, R. C. (1996). Research foundations to support wide reading. In V. Greaney (Ed.), *Promoting reading in developing countries* (pp. 55–77). Newark, DE: International Reading Association.

Anderson, R. C., & Freebody, P. (1981). Vocabulary knowledge. In J. Guthrie (ed.), *Comprehension and Teaching: Research Reviews* (pp. 77–117). Newark, DE: International Reading Association.

Anderson, R. C., & Nagy, W. E. (1992, Winter). The vocabulary conundrum. *American Educator, 16,* 14–18, 44–47.

Anderson, R. C., & Pearson, P. D. (1984). A schema-theoretic view of basic processes in reading. In P. D. Pearson, R. Barr, M. L. Kamil, & P. Mosenthal (Eds.), *Handbook of reading research* (pp. 255–291). New York: Longman.

Anderson, R. C., Wilson, P. T., & Fielding, L. G. (1988). Growth in reading and how children spend their time outside of school. *Reading Research Quarterly, 23,* 285–303.

Au, K. H. (1980). Participation structures in a reading lesson with Hawaiian children: Analysis of a culturally appropriate instructional event. *Anthropology and Education Quarterly, 11,* 91–115.

Au, K. H. (2002). Multicultural Factors and the Effective Instruction of Students of Diverse Backgrounds. In A. E. Farstrup & S. J. Samuels (Eds.), *What research has to say about reading instruction* (pp. 392–413). Newark, DE: International Reading Association.

Baker, S. K., Simmons, D. C., & Kameenui, E. J. (1995). *Vocabulary acquisition: Synthesis of the research.* (Tech. Rep. No. 13). Eugene: University of Oregon, National Center to Improve the Tools for Educators.

Bamford, R. A., & Kristo, J. V. (2003). *Making facts come alive: Choosing & using nonfiction literature K–8.* Norwood, MA: Christopher-Gordon.

Beaver, J. (1997). *Developmental reading assessment.* Parsippany, NJ: Celebration Press.

Beck, I. L., McKeown, M. G., & Kucan, L. (2002). *Bringing words to life: Robust vocabulary instruction.* New York: Guilford Press.

Becker, W. C. (1977). Teaching reading and language to the disadvantaged—What we have learned from field research. *Harvard Educational Review, 47,* 518–543.

Biemiller, A. (1977). Relationships between oral reading rates for letters, words, and simple text in the development of reading achievement. *Reading Research Quarterly, 13,* 223–253.

Blachowicz, C., & Fisher, P. J. (2002). *Teaching vocabulary in all classrooms* (2nd ed.). Upper Saddle River, NJ: Merrill Prentice Hall.

Blevins, W. (2001). *Building fluency: Lessons and strategies for reading success*. New York: Scholastic.

Block, C. C., Gambrell, L. B., & Pressley, M. (Eds.). (2002). *Improving comprehension instruction: rethinking research, theory, and classroom practice*. San Francisco: Jossey-Bass.

Block, C. C., & Pressley, M. (2003). Best practices in comprehension instruction. In L. M. Morrow, L. B. Gambrell, & M. Pressley (Eds.), *Best practices in literacy instruction* (2nd ed., pp. 111–126). New York: Guilford Press.

Block, C. C., Rodgers, L. L., & Johnson, R. B. (2004). *Comprehension process instruction: Creating reading success in grades K–3*. New York: Guilford Press.

Bransford J. A., Brown, A., & Cocking, R. (1999). *How people learn: Brain, mind, experience, and school* (National Research Council). Washington, DC: National Academy Press.

Britton, J. N.(1970). *Language and learning*. Coral Gables, FL: University of Miami Press.

Brown, R., Cazden, C., & Bellugi-Klima, U.(1968). The child's grammar from one to three. In J. P. Hill (Ed.), *Minnesota Symposium on child development*. Minneapolis: University of Minnesota Press.

Cazden, C. (1988). *Classroom discourse: The language of teaching and learning*. Portsmouth, NH: Heinemann.

Chomsky, N. (1969). *Aspects of a theory of syntax*. Cambridge, MA: MIT Press.

Clay, M. M. (1976). Early childhood and cultural diversity in New Zealand. *Reading Teacher, 29*, 333-342.

Clay, M. M. (1991) *Becoming literate: The construction of inner control*. Portsmouth, NH: Heinemann.

Clay, M. M. (1993). *An observation survey of early literacy achievement*. Portsmouth, NH: Heinemann.

Clay, M. M.(2000). *Running records for classroom teachers*. Portsmouth, NH: Heinemann.

Cole, A. D. (2003) *Knee to knee, eye to eye: Circling in on comprehension*. Portsmouth, NH: Heinemann.

Cole, A. D. (2004). *When reading begins: the teacher's role in decoding, comprehension, and fluency*. Portsmouth, NH: Heinemann.

Cummins, J.(1979). Linguistic interdependence and the educational development of bilingual children. *Review of Educational Research, 49*, 222–251.

Dale, E. (1965). Vocabulary measurement: Techniques and major findings. *Elementary English, 42*, 82-88.

Delpit, L. (1995). *Other people's children*. New York: New Press.

Dorn, L. J., French, C., & Jones, T. (1998). *Apprenticeship in literacy: Transitions across reading and writing*. Portland, ME: Stenhouse.

Dorn, L. J., & Soffos, C. (2001) *Shaping literate minds: Developing self-regulated learners*. Portland, ME: Stenhouse.

Dowhower, S. (1987). Effects of repeated reading on second grade transitional reader's fluency and comprehension. *Reading Research Quarterly, 22*, 389–406.

Duffy, G. G. (2003). *Explaining reading: A resource for teaching concepts, skills, and strategies*. New York: Guilford Press.

Duke, N. K., & Pearson, P. D. (2002). Effective practices for developing reading comprehension. In A. E. Farstrup and S. J. Samuels (Eds.), *What research has to say about reading instruction* (3rd ed., pp. 205–242). Newark, DE: International Reading Association.

Feitelson, D., & Goldstein, Z. (1986). Patterns of book ownership and reading to young children in Israeli school-oriented and nonschool-oriented families. *Reading Teacher, 39,* 924–930.

Ferreiro, E., & Teberosky, A. (1982). *Literacy before schooling.* Portsmouth, NH: Heinemann.

Fleisher, L., Jenkins, J., & Pany, D. (1979). Effects on poor readers' comprehension of training in rapid decoding. *Reading Research Quarterly, 20,* 553–565.

Fountas, I.C., & Pinnell, G. S. (1996). *Guided reading: Good first teaching for all children.* Portsmouth, NH: Heinemann.

Fountas, I. C., & Pinnell, G. S. (1999). *Voices on word matters: Learning about phonics and spelling in the literacy classroom,* (Eds.). Portsmouth, NH: Heinemann.

Freeman, D. E., & Freeman, Y. S. (2004). *Essential linguistics: What you need to know to teach reading ESL, spelling, phonics, grammar.* Portsmouth, NH: Heinemann.

Fukkink, R. G., & de Glopper, K. (1998). Effects of instruction in deriving word meaning from context: A meta-analysis. *Review of Educational Research, 68.*

Garton, A., & Pratt, C. (1998) *Learning to be literate: The development of spoken and written language* (2nd ed.). Malden, MA: Blackwell.

Gillet, J. W., & Temple, C. (2000). *Understanding reading Problems* (5th ed.). New York: Longman.

Goodman, Y. M., & Goodman, K. S. (2004). To err is human: Learning about language processes by analyzing miscues. In R. B. Ruddell, & N. J. Unrau (Eds.), *Theoretical models and process of reading* (5th ed.) (pp. 620–639). Newark, DE: International Reading Association.

Graves, M. F. (1986). Vocabulary learning and instruction. In E. Z. Rothkopf (Ed.), *Review of Research in Education* (Vol. 13, pp. 49–89). Washington, DC: American Educational Research Association.

Graves, M. F. (2000). A vocabulary program to complement and bolster a middle-grade comprehension program. In B. M. Taylor, M. F. Graves, & P. van den Broek (Eds.), *Reading for meaning: Fostering comprehension in the middle grades* (pp. 116–135). New York: teachers college Press; Newark, DE: International Reading Association.

Graves, M. F., Brunetti, G. J., & Slater, W. H. (1982). The reading vocabularies of primary-grade children of varying geographic and social backgrounds. In J. A. Harris & L. A. Harris (Eds.), *New inquiries in reading research and instruction* (pp. 99–104). Rochester, NY: National Reading Conference.

Graves, M. F, & Graves, B. (1994). *Scaffolding reading experiences: Designs for student success.* Norwood, MA: Christopher Gordon.

Graves, M. F., & Slater, W. H. (1987). *The development of reading vocabularies in rural disadvantaged students, inner-city disadvantaged students, and middle-class suburban students.* Paper presented at the meeting of the American Educational Research Association, Washington, DC.

Graves, M. F., & Watts-Taffe, S. M. (2002). The place of word consciousness in a research-based vocabulary program. In A. E. Farstrup and S. J. Samuels (Eds.), *What research has to say about reading instruction* (3rd ed., pp. 140–165). Newark, DE: International Reading Association.

Halliday, M. A. K. (1975). *Learning how to mean: Exploration in the development of language.* London: Edward Arnold.

Hart, B., & Risley, T. R. (1995). *Meaningful differences in the everyday experiences of young American children*. Baltimore: Paul H. Brookes.

Harvey, S., & Goudvis, A. (2000). *Strategies that work: Teaching comprehension to enhance understanding*. York, ME: Stenhouse.

Hasbrouck, J. E., & Tindal, G. (1992). Curriculum-based oral reading fluency norms for students in grades 2 through 5. *Teaching Exceptional Children, 24*, 41–44.

Henderson, E. (1986). Understanding children's knowledge of written language. In D. Yaden & S. Templeton (Eds.), *Metalinguistic awareness and beginning literacy: Conceptualizing what it means to read and write* (pp. 65–78). Portsmouth, NH: Heinemann.

Herman, P. (1985). The effect of repeated readings on reading rate, speech pauses, and word recognition accuracy. *Reading Research Quarterly, 20*, 553-565.

Hiebert, E. (1986). Issues related to home influences on young children's print-related development. In D. Yaden & S. Templeton (Eds.), *Metalinguistic awareness and beginning literacy: Conceptualizing what it means to read and write* (pp. 145–158), Portsmouth, NH: Heinemann.

Holdaway, D. (1979). *The foundations of literacy*. Portsmouth, NH: Heinemann.

Holdaway, D. (1980). *Independence in reading*. Portsmouth, NH: Heinemann.

Irwin, J. W. (1991). *Teaching reading comprehension processes* (2nd ed.). Boston: Allyn and Bacon.

Johns, J. L., & Berglund, R. L. (2002). *Fluency: Questions, answers, evidence-based strategies*. Dubuque, IA: Kendall/Hunt.

Johnston, P. H. (2004). *Choice words: How our language affects children's learning*. Portland, ME: Stenhouse.

Karmiloff, K., & Karmiloff-Smith, A. (2001). *Pathways to language: From fetus to adolescent*. Cambridge, MA: Harvard University Press.

Keene, E. O., & Zimmerman, S. (1997). *Mosaic of thought: Teaching comprehension in a reader's workshop*. Portsmouth, NH: Heinemann.

Kristo, J. V., & Bamford, R. A. (2004). *Nonfiction in focus: A comprehensive framework for helping students become independent readers and writers of nonfiction, K–6*. New York: Scholastic.

Kucan, L., & Beck, I. L. (1997). Thinking aloud and reading comprehension research: Inquiry, instruction and social interaction. *Review of Educational Research, 67*, 271–299.

Kuhn, M. R., & Stahl, S. A. (2000). *Fluency: A review of developmental and remedial practices*. Ann Arbor, MI: Center for the Improvement of Early Reading Achievement.

LaBerge, D., & Samuels, S. J. (1974). Toward a theory of automatic information processing in reading. *Cognitive Psychology, 6*, 293–323.

Lapp, D., Flood, J., & Roser, N. (2000). Still standing: Timeless strategies for teaching the language arts. In D. S. Strickland & L. M. Morrow (Eds.), *Beginning reading and writing*. New York: Teachers College Press.

Leslie, L. & Caldwell, J. (2001). *Qualitative reading inventory–3*. New York: Longman.

Lindfors, J. W. (1991). *Children's language and learning* (2nd ed.). Boston: Allyn and Bacon.

Lyon, A., & Moore, P. (2003). *Sound systems: Explicit, systematic phonics in early literacy contexts*. Portland, ME: Stenhouse.

McCarrier, A., Pinnell, G. S., & Fountas, I. C. (2000). *Interactive writing: How language and literacy come together, K–2*. Portsmouth, NH: Heinemann.

McLaughlin, M. (2003). *Guided comprehension in the primary grades*. Newark, DE: International Reading Association.

Moats, L. C. (2000). *Speech to print: Language essentials for teachers*. Baltimore: Paul H. Brookes.

Mooney, M. (1990). *Reading to, with, and by children*. Katonah, NY: Richard C. Owen.

Moore, P. (2003). Choosing quality nonfiction literature: Aspects of selection for emergent, early and transitional readers. In R. A. Bamford and J. V. Kristo (Eds.), *Making facts come alive: Choosing & using nonfiction literature K–8* (pp. 97–118). Norwood, MA: Christopher-Gordon.

Morrow, L. M. (1992). The impact of a literature-based program on literacy achievement, use of literature, and attitudes of children from minority backgrounds. *Reading Research Quarterly*, 27, 251-275.

Nagy, W. E. (1988). *Teaching vocabulary to improve reading comprehension*. Newark, DE: International Reading Association.

Nagy, W. E., & Anderson, R. C. (1984). How many words are there in printed school English? *Reading Research Quarterly*, 19, 303–330.

Nagy, W. E., & Herman, P. A. (1987). Depth and breadth of vocabulary knowledge: Implications for acquisition and instruction. In M. G. McKeown & M. E. Curtis (Eds.), *The nature of vocabulary acquisition*. Hillsdale, NJ: Erlbaum.

Nagy, W. E., Herman, P. A., & Anderson, R. C. (1985). Learning words from context. *Reading Research Quarterly*, 20, 233–253.

National Institute of Child Health and Human Development (NICHHD). (2000a, December). Report of the National Reading Panel. *Teaching children to read: An evidence-based assessment of the scientific research literature on reading and its implications for reading instruction* (NIH Publication No. 00-4754). Washington, DC: Author.

National Institute of Child Health and Human Development (NICHHD). (2000b, December). Report of The National Reading Panel, Reports of the Subgroups. *Teaching children to read: An evidence-based assessment of the scientific research literature on reading and its implications for reading instruction* (NIH Publication No. 00-4754). Washington, DC: Author.

New Zealand Department of Education (1994).

Osborn, J., Lehr, F., & Hiebert, E. H. (2003). *A focus on fluency*. In the Research-Based Practices in Early Reading series. Honolulu, HI: Regional Educational Laboratory at Pacific Resources for Education and Learning.

Owocki, G. (2003) *Comprehension: Strategic instruction for K–3 students*. Portsmouth, NH: Heinemann.

Paris, S. G., & Lindauer, B. K. (1976). The role of inference in children's comprehension and memory. *Cognitive Psychology*, 8, 217–227.

Parkes, B. (2000). *Read it again! Revisiting shared reading*. Portland, ME: Stenhouse.

Pearson, P. D., Roehler, L. R., Dole, J. A., & Duffy, G. G. (1992). Developing expertise in reading comprehension. In A. E. Farstrup and S. J. Samuels (Eds.), *What research has to say about reading instruction* (2nd ed., pp. 145–199). Newark, DE: International Reading Association.

Peterson, R. (1992). *Life in a crowded place: Making a learning community*. Portsmouth, NH: Heinemann.

Piaget, J. (1955) *The language and thought of the child*. New York: Meridian.

Pinnell, G. S., Pikulski, J.J., Wixson, K.K., Campbell, J. R., Gough, P.B., & Beatty A.S. (1995). *Listening to children read aloud: Data from NAEP's integrated reading performance record (IRPR) at grade 4*. Washington, DC: National Center for Educational Statistics.

Pressley, M. (2000). What should comprehension instruction be the instruction of? In M. Kamil, P. Mosenthal, P. D. Pearson, & R. Barr (Eds.), *Handbook of reading research* (Vol. 3, pp. 545–562). Hillsdale, NJ: Erlbaum.

Pressley, M. (2002). *Reading instruction that works: The case for balanced teaching*. New York: Guilford Press.

RAND Reading Study Group. (2002). *Reading for understanding. Toward an R & D program in reading comprehension*. Santa Monica, CA: RAND Science & Technology Policy Institute.

Raphael, T. E., & Hiebert, E. H. (1996). *Creating an integrated approach to literacy instruction*. Fort Worth, TX: Harcourt Brace.

Rasinski, T. V. (1990). *The effects of cued phrase boundaries in texts*. Bloomington, IN: ERIC Clearinghouse on Reading and Communication skills. (ERIC Document Reproduction Service No. 313 689)

Rasinski, T. V. (1995). Fast Start: A parental involvement reading program for primary grade students. In W. Linek & E. Sturtevant (Eds.), *Generation of literacy: Seventeenth Yearbook of the College Reading Association* (pp. 301–312). Harrisonburg, VA: College Reading Association.

Rasinski, T. V. (2003). *The fluent reader: Oral reading strategies for building word recognition, fluency, and comprehension*. New York, NY: Scholastic.

Rasinski, T. V., & Padak, N. (2001). *From phonics to fluency: Effective teaching of decoding and reading fluency in the elementary school*. New York: Longman.

Reutzel, D. R., Camperell, K., & Smith, J. A. (2002). Hitting the wall: Helping struggling readers comprehend. In C. C. Block, L. B. Gambrell, & M. Pressley (Eds.), *Improving comprehension instruction: Rethinking research, theory, and classroom practice* (2nd ed., pp.321–353). San Francisco: Jossey-Bass.

Reutzel, D. R., & Hollingsworth, P. M. (1993). Effects of fluency training on second graders' reading comprehension. *Journal of Educational Research*, *86*, 147–150.

Rosenblatt, L. M. (1995). *Literature as exploration*. New York: Modern Language Association of America.

Samuels, S. J. (1979). The method of repeated reading. *The Reading Teacher*, *32*, 403-408.

Samuels, S. J. (2002). Reading fluency: Its development and assessment. In A. E. Farstrup & S. J Samuels (Eds.), *What research has to say about reading instruction* (3rd ed.). Newark, DE: International Reading Association.

Samuels, S. J., Schermer N., & Reinking, D. (1992). Reading fluency: Techniques for making decoding automatic. In S. J. Samuels & A. E. Farstrup (Eds.), *What research has to say about reading instruction* (2nd ed., pp. 124–144), Newark, DE: International Reading Association.

Schreiber, P. A. (1987). Prosody and structure in children's syntactic processing. In R. Horowitz & S. J. Samuels (Eds.), *Comprehending oral and written language* (pp. 243–270). New York: Academic Press.

Sipe, L. R. (2000). The construction of literacy understanding by first and second graders in oral response to picture storybook read-alouds. *Reading Research Quarterly*, *35*, 252-275.

Sipe, L. R. (2002). Talking back and taking over: Young children's expressive engagement during storybook read-alouds. *The Reading Teacher*, *55*, 476–483.

Skinner, B. F. (1957) *Verbal behavior*. New York: Appleton.

Snow, C. E., Burns, M. S., & Griffin, P. (Eds.). (1998). *Preventing reading difficulties in young children*. Washington, DC: National Academy Press.

Stahl, K. A. D. (2004). Proof, practice, and promise: Comprehension strategy instruction in the primary grades. *Reading Teacher, 57,* 598–609.

Stahl, S. A. (1998). Four questions about vocabulary. In C. R. Hynd (Ed.), *Learning from text across conceptual domains* (pp. 73–94). Hillsdale, NJ: Erlbaum.

Stanovich, K. E. (1986). Matthew effects in reading: Some consequences of individual differences in the acquisition of literacy. *Reading Research Quarterly, 21,* 360-406.

Steinbeck, J. (1961). *The winter of our discontent.* New York: Penguin Books.

Sternberg, R. J. (1987). Most vocabulary is learned from context. In M. G. McKeown & M. E. Curtis (Eds.), *The nature of vocabulary acquisition* (pp. 89–105). Hillsdale, NJ: Erlbaum.

Su, Y. F., Samuels, S. J., & Flom, R. (1999). *Indicators of automaticity in decoding.* Unpublished manuscript, University of Minnesota, Minneapolis.

Sulzby, E., & Teale, W. (1991). Emergent literacy. In R. Barr, M. Kamil, P. Mosenthal, & P. D. Pearson (Eds.), *Handbook of reading research* (Vol. 2, pp. 727–758). Hillsdale, NJ: Erlbaum.

Sweet, A. P., & Snow, C. (2002). Reconceptualizing reading instruction. In C. C. Block, L. B. Gambrell, & M. Pressley (Eds.), *Improving comprehension instruction: Rethinking research, theory, and classroom practice.* San Francisco: Jossey-Bass.

Tabors, P. O. (1997). *One child, two languages.* Baltimore: Paul Brookes.

Taylor, B. M., Frye, B. J., & Maruyama, G. M. (1990). Time spent reading and reading growth. *American Educational Research Journal, 27,* 351–362.

Thompkins, G. E., & Blanchfield, C. (2004). *Teaching vocabulary: 50 creative strategies, grades K–12.* Upper Saddle River, NJ: Merrill Prentice Hall.

Thurlow, R., & van den Broek, P. (1997). Automaticity and inference generation. *Reading and Writing Quarterly, 13,* 165–184.

Vygotsky, L. S. (1978). *Mind in society: The development of psychological processes.* Cambridge, MA: Harvard University Press.

Wells, G. (1986). *The meaning makers: Children learning language and using language to learn.* Portsmouth, NH: Heinemann.

White, T. G., Graves, M. F., & Slater, W. H. (1990). Development of recognition and reading vocabularies in diverse sociolinguistic and educational settings. *Journal of Educational Psychology, 82,* 281–290.

Wilhelm, J. D. (1997). *You gotta be the book.* New York: Teachers College Press.

Wilhelm, J. D. (2001). *Improving comprehension with think-aloud strategies: Modeling what good readers do.* New York: Scholastic.

Wood, D. (1998). *How children think and learn* (2nd ed.). Cambridge, MA: Blackwell.

Zaprorzhets, A. V., & Elkonin, D. B. (Eds.). (1971). *The psychology of preschool children.* Cambridge, MA: MIT Press.

Zeno, S. M., Ivens, S. H., Millard, R. T., & Duvvuri, R. (1995). *The educator's word frequency guide.* New York: Touchstone Applied Science Associates.

Children's Books Cited

Ajmera, M. & Regan, M. V. (2000). *Let the games begin*. Watertown, MA: Charlesbridge.

Akass, S. (2000). *The great escape*. Rigby Literacy Series. Barrington, IL: Rigby.

Arnosky, J. (2002). *All about frogs*. New York: Scholastic.

Bang, M. (1999). *When Sophie gets angry—very, very angry*. New York: Blue Sky Press.

Beeler, S. B. (1998). *Throw your tooth on the roof*. New York: Houghton Mifflin.

Berger, M. (1994). *Those fabulous frogs*. New York: Newbridge.

Brandenburg, J. (1996). *Scruffy: A wolf finds his place in the pack*. New York: Walker and Company.

Bunting, E. (1994). *Night tree*. New York: Harcourt Brace.

Cowley, J. (1988). *The surprise*. Bothell, WA: The Wright Group.

Cowley, J. (1990). *Mrs. wishy-washy*. Bothell, WA: The Wright Group.

Cronin, D. (2000). *Click, clack, moo cows that type*. New York: Simon & Schuster Books for Young readers.

Dorling kindersley merriam webster's children's dictionary. (2000) New York: Dorling Kindersley.

Freeman, D. (1978). *A pocket for corduroy*. New York: Viking.

Gibson, A. (1994). *There's a hole in my pocket*. New York: Scholastic.

Henkes, K. (2000). Wemberly worried. New York: Greenwillow.

Huck, C. (1989). *Princess furball*. New York: Greenwillow Books.

Hutchins, P. (1968). *Rosie's walk*. New York: Scholastic.

Martin, B., Jr. (1996). *Brown bear, brown bear, what do you see?* New York: Holt.

Petty, K. (1989). *Guinea pigs*. New York: Gloucester Press.

Raffi (1988). *Wheels on the bus*. New York: Crown.

Raffi (1992). *Baby beluga*. New York: Crown.

Randell, B. (1994). *Sally's friends*. Barrington, IL: Rigby.

Rey, M., & Rey, H. A. (1966). *Curious george goes to the hospital*. Boston: Houghton Mifflin.

Rosen, M. (2002). *We're going on a bear hunt*. New York: Aladdin Paperbacks.

Royston, A. (1991) *Frog*. New York: Lodestar Books.

Scieszka, J. (1989). *The true story of the 3 little pigs. New York: Viking*.

Snowball, D. (1995). *Chickens*. New York: Mondo.

Stevens, J. (1995) *Tops & bottoms*. New York: Harcourt Brace.

Steward, S. (1997). *The gardener*. New York: Scholastic.

Taback, S. (1997) *I know an old lady who swallowed a fly*. New York: Viking.

Viorst, J. (1994). *The alphabet from z to a (with much confusion on the way)*. New York: Macmillan.

Williams, R. L. (1994). *The bear went over the mountain*. Cypress, CA: Creative Teaching Press.

Index

A

accuracy, 124
    assessment, 59–61
    reading and, 54–55
Adams, Marilyn, 127
Ajmera, Maya and Michael Regan
    Let the Games Begin, 86
Akass, Susan
    Great Escape, The, 104–105
All About Frogs, (Arnosky), 86–88, 100–102,
    117–120, 136–137
Allen, Janet, 49
Anderson, Carl, 21
Apprenticeship in Literacy, (Dorn, French, and
    Jones), 66
Arnosky, Jim
    All About Frogs, 86–88, 100–102, 117–120,
    136–137
assessment
    accuracy, 59–61
    expression, 62–64
    oral reading fluency, 57–59
    reading rate, 61–62

B

Baby Beluga, (Raffi) 94
Bang, Molly
    When Sophie Gets Angry—Very, Very Angry,
    111
Bear Went over the Mountain, The, (Williams),94
Beaver, Joetta, *Developmental Reading Inventory*, 57
Beck, Isabel, 39, 43, 45–47, 77, 108, 116
Beeler, Selby
    Throw Your Tooth on the Roof, 86
behaviorists, 17
Brandenburg, Jim
    Scruffy: A Wolf Finds His Place in the Pack, 26,
    96
Britton, James, 88
    Language and Learning, 22

Brown Bear, Brown Bear, What Do You See?,
    (Martin, Jr.), 8, 9
Bunting, Eve
    Fly Away Home, 8
    Night Tree, 21
    Wednesday's Surprise, 8

C

Cazden, Courtney, 19
Chickens, (Snowball), 9
Chomsky, Noam, 17
classroom behavior, talk and, 22
classroom coaching model, 160–161
Clay, Marie, 128–129
    Running Records for Classroom Teachers, 58
cognitive development, 18
Cole, Ardith, 103–104
    Knee to Knee, Eye to Eye, 103–104
comprehension, 124
    comprehending, versus, 28–29
    defined, 27–28
    research, 29–32, 91–93
    talk, role of and, 35
comprehension instruction
    classroom context for, 33–35
    first grade, 96–97
    kindergarten, 95–96
    model of, 36–37, 93
    preschool, 94–95
    research, 32–38
    second grade, 97–105
    think-aloud, 35–36
comprehensive early literacy program defined,
    66–67
concept-based vocabulary, 109
    See also vocabulary
concepts, vocabulary and, 44
    See also vocabulary
constructivist theories, 18
content area studies, 117

New Essentials for Teaching Reading in PreK–2

New Essentials for Teaching Reading in PreK–2